BARRON'S PARENTING KEYS

KEYS TO PARENTING MULTIPLES

Second Edition

D0912678

Karen Kerkhoff Gromada,
M.S.N., R.N., I.B.C.L.C.

Mary C. Hurlburt, C.C.C.C.

BARRON'S

Cover photo by The Stock Market

DEDICATION

To our husbands, Joe and Barry, and our children, who gave us the support and freedom to write this book.

All inquiries should be addressed to:
Barron's Educational Series, Inc.
250 Wireless Boulevard
Hauppauge, New York 11788
http://www.barronseduc.com

Library of Congress Catalog Card No.: 00-056453

International Standard Book No. 0-7641-1293-7

Library of Congress Cataloging-in-Publication Data
Gromada, Karen Kerkhoff.
  Keys to parenting multiples / Karen Kerkhoff Gromada, Mary C. Hurlburt.—2nd ed.
      p.   cm.—(Barron's parenting keys)
  Rev. ed. of: Keys to parenting twins. c1992.
  Includes bibliographical references and index.
  ISBN 0-7641-1293-7
      1. Multiple birth.   2. Child rearing.   3. Infants—Care.
  4. Pregnancy.   I. Hurlburt, Mary C.   II. Gromada, Karen
  Kerkhoff. Keys to parenting twins.   III. Title.   IV. Series.

HQ777.35. G76   2001
649'.144—dc21   00-056453

PRINTED IN THE UNITED STATES OF AMERICA
98765432

CONTENTS

INTRODUCTION

Welcome to the exciting world of multiple parenting. Multiples add a new and very special dimension to the dynamics of a family. Be assured that whatever emotions you feel when you discover you are expecting babies instead of a single baby, they are normal! Almost all prospective parents of multiples experience both positive and negative feelings. You may be excited one day or hour and petrified the next.

This is a wonderful time to be having multiples. If you are expecting twins you have a better chance of delivering full-term babies with acceptable birth weights than even 10 years ago. With early detection and appropriate prenatal care, many higher-order multiples are also born closer to term. Plus, the survival rate and normal development for preterm, low-birth-weight babies has increased tremendously.

Parenting multiples is not the same as parenting children close in age. From the beginning parenting multiples is more complicated than parenting a single child. Multiple pregnancies are monitored more closely. Bonding, or falling in love, with two or more babies is different from bonding with only one.

Multiples are fascinating. Everyone is intrigued by twins, triplets, or more. As parents of multiples you feel special and you *are*.

Parents' personal growth also is enormous. You learn to organize and prioritize as you discard all the nonessential elements of your life. Multiples teach parents tolerance and empathy for others in unusual situations. When you handle new challenges each day, you realize you can handle almost anything. Parents develop a sense of humor, because they need it. You laugh because your multiples do the funniest things. On frantic days, humor may be all that holds you together. You have a different point of reference for raising these children. The issue of the multiple-to-multiple relationship will enter into most parenting decisions you make about one or another. The uniqueness of being one of multiples remains a vital and intimate part of their identities and parent decision-making for life. Without appropriate resources, however, parents are left to "reinvent the wheel" to discover multiple-parenting skills.

Our goal in writing this book is to provide support, offer practical suggestions, and encourage you to celebrate the individuality of your family and that of each of your children. We have worked with thousands of parents of multiples since our own were born. From 1981 through 1992, we published *Double Talk*—an international parent-information-sharing newsletter. We have worked and continue to work through support groups and speaking engagements. This book is a compilation of our personal experiences and the information we have gleaned from these parents. We've learned that certain situations frequently arise with the birth of multiples, yet each family is still unique.

One often-asked question is, "Is there life after multiples?" Yes, there is. Mary has moved on to a career in finance and is often asked to consult on issues of parenting multiples. Karen is a labor relations/management consultant and still counsels many parents of multiples every year. She also frequently makes presentations to health professionals on multiple pregnancy issues. Our twins are now college graduates with lives of their own.

Parenting multiples is an experience of a lifetime, and being a parent of twins, triplets, or more remains part of your identity. You are part of a select group privileged to enjoy this unique "nature versus nurture" parenting experience, addressing the question of whether our genetic makeup or environmental influences have more of an impact on the adults we become. Enjoy it! We still are!

Mary C. Hurlburt, C.C.C.C.

Karen Kerkhoff Gromada, M.S.N., R.N., I.B.C.L.C.

1

CONCEIVING MULTIPLES

The diagnosis is definite. More than one baby is growing inside you. How did this happen? What leads to the conception of twins, triplets, or more? How did you come to be the lucky one expecting multiples? This Key discusses how multiples develop and who is more likely to conceive them.

Conception

The incidence of multiple births increased considerably during the last two decades of the twentieth century mostly as a result of the advances in *assisted reproductive technology* (ART). Between 1980 and 1999, twin births increased by more than 50 percent, and the number of higher-order multiple births rose more than 400 percent. In spite of this monumental leap in higher-order multiple births, triplets and other higher-order multiples represent less than one-tenth of 1 percent of the birth rate in the United States. The vast majority of multiple births continue to be twin births, and the process that results in conceiving any number of multiples still is referred to as "twinning."

Identical twinning. Science is not certain why identical twinning occurs, but it is known how it occurs. Identical multiples begin life the same as any single infant. One sperm fertilizes one egg (ovum). Fertilization, the joining of the sperm and ovum, results in a new single cell called the *zygote*. The zygote then begins to rapidly divide—first into two cells, then four, eight, sixteen, and so on. At some point in the process of this early cell division, half of the zygote's cells completely separate from the other half. Now there are two zygotes, which are genetically identical, instead of one.

For almost 75 percent of identical twin sets, the single zygote implants in the lining of the uterus before separating into two different zygotes, and these identical twins share one placenta. These identical multiples also share the outer layer of the amniotic sac, which many refer to as the "bag of waters." The shared outer layer of the sac is the *chorion*. The inner layer of the amniotic sac is called the *amnion,* but few twins also share a common amnion. To get an idea of how there can be one chorion but two amnions, picture a balloon as the chorion and then imagine the amnions as two water balloons inside it.

In 1 to 2 percent of identical twin sets, the babies share an amnion as well as the chorion, so both babies move within the same fluid-filled sac. Sharing the same sac increases risks for babies, so obstetric care providers look for separation of amnions when they review ultrasound scans for single-placenta multiple pregnancies. Also, certain pregnancy and birth interventions may be suggested to lessen the chance of complications for the babies. (See Keys 4 through 7 for information about reducing risks.)

About 25 percent of identical sets have separate placentas. When the original zygote splits to form two zygotes and they travel down the fallopian tube toward the uterus before implantation, each zygote finds its own implantation spot in the uterine lining. Because of this earlier split with separate implantation, these identical sets have separate placentas.

Another name for identical twins is *monozygotic* twins, meaning "one-zygote twins." Since each monozygotic twin develops from the original fertilized egg, they have 100 percent of their genetic material in common. This is why identical twins are the same sex, and why their physical appearance and temperaments tend to be so similar. Identical twins may be difficult to tell apart until a person knows each well. Although it is a rare occurrence, triplets, quadruplets, or quintuplets may result from a single zygote.

Fraternal twinning. Fraternal twins result when two separate eggs (ova) are released at ovulation and are fertilized by two different sperm in the fallopian tube(s). These two different zygotes travel to and implant separately in the uterine lining. Each always develops a separate placenta and amniotic sac. Sometimes the two zygotes implant next to one another and one edge of their placentas fuse, so they may appear to share a single placenta when there are actually two. Laboratory personnel can examine a placenta to determine whether it is actually two that have fused. Let your obstetric care provider know that you want the placenta examined, since this testing is not routinely done in all areas. For more information on determining twin type, see Key 19.

Another name for fraternal twins is *dizygotic* twins, meaning "two-zygote twins." Dizygotic twins are siblings who happen to inhabit the uterus at the same time and share the same birthday. These twins are as alike or unalike as any siblings, since they have about 50 percent of their genetic material in common. Fraternal twins may be the same or different genders, and they may look very similar or very different as with any other brothers and sisters.

Higher-order multiples. Triplets and other higher-order multiples, who sometimes are referred to as *supertwins*, may be all identical (monozygotic) or all fraternal (dizygotic/polyzygotic), or they may result from a combination of identical and fraternal twinning. The highest number of known identical multiples in one set are the Dionne quintuplets of Canada. It is not unusual for higher-order multiple sets to include a set of identical twins plus one or more fraternal infants.

Who Has Multiples?

The incidence of *monozygotic twinning* is about the same for women of every ethnic group and culture. The rate remains stable at about 1 per 250 live births. Neither heredity nor any other factor seems to influence its occurrence. However, there are reports of several sets of identical twins within some extended families, which is a phenomenon unlikely to occur by chance alone. Also, in vitro fertilization (IVF) appears to affect monozygotic twinning.

Many factors influence *dizygotic twinning* rates. All are related to the releasing of more than one mature egg at ovulation. A woman is more likely to produce two eggs and conceive dizygotic twins if she

1. has a family history of fraternal twins on her mother's side
2. has already given birth to dizygotic twins
3. conceives after 35 years of age (unrelated to prior pregnancies or ART)
4. has had several other pregnancies
5. conceives within the first three months of marriage
6. conceives during her first spontaneous menstrual cycle after discontinuing birth control pills.

Black women have a higher naturally occurring dizygotic twinning rate than whites, who have a higher rate than Asians.

The dizygotic twinning rate has greatly increased in the last few decades. In the 1970s, twins comprised 1.4 percent of the live births in the United States. That percentage has increased, so that now about 2.4 percent of live births are twins. Most of these twins are fraternal sets. Although 1 percent may not seem like a tremendous increase when viewed as part of the total number of births, this number reflects an almost 40 percent increase in the number of twin births between 1980 and the mid-1990s. Some of the increase is due to the greater number of women postponing childbearing until after thirty, but the development of fertility-enhancing ART accounts for most of the increase.

Women who receive what are called ovarian stimulation medications have a significantly higher rate of dizygotic twinning, because these medications promote the production and release of more than one egg per menstrual cycle. Such medication may be given alone or in combination with medication that helps eggs mature and medication that helps prepare the lining of the uterus for implantation. Medication also may be combined with other techniques that enhance fertility, such as intrauterine insemination (IUI), in vitro fertilization (IVF), gamete or zygote intrafallopian transfer (GIFT/ZIFT), and so on.

When treatment involves ovarian stimulation medications, especially gonadotropins, about 20 percent of any resulting pregnancies will be multiple pregnancies compared with a 1 to 2 percent twin pregnancy rate for the general population. Of course, it also is possible for a single zygote, conceived after a woman took an ovulatory induction agent, to split and form identical twins.

The increase in higher-order multiples is due almost exclusively to the use of gonadotropins for ovarian stimulation with or without additional techniques. Before the advances in ART, the birth of higher-order multiples was a rare event. Only one of 7,000 births was a triplet birth. Quadruplets could be expected about once every 600,000 births and quintuplets appeared once in 47,000,000.

ART affected the birth rate of higher-order multiples so dramatically that by 1980 one of 2,700 infants was a higher-order multiple, and by the mid-1990s one of 655 was a part of a higher-order multiple birth. The birth rate of higher-order multiples increased about 350 percent between 1980 and the turn of the century.

ART in the Twenty-first Century

The low rate of naturally occurring twins and higher-order multiples would suggest that the human female is designed for single-infant pregnancies. Reproductive medicine specialists are constantly working to improve ovarian stimulation medications and learn more about their use with the goal of helping couples achieve single-infant pregnancy while avoiding the risks of multiple pregnancy. Specialists also are beginning to *limit the number* of gametes (unfertilized egg and sperm) or zygotes/embryos (fertilized eggs at various stages of cell division) transferred during ART procedures, which should limit the number of higher-order multiple pregnancies. Also, improvements in IVF technology now allow specialists to watch zygotes develop longer so they can transfer "healthier" zygotes.

This is just the beginning for ART science, and increases in multiple pregnancies, particularly twin pregnancies, are likely to continue for several more decades. Of course, future technology has little meaning for a couple already pregnant with two or more!

2

PARENT AND DOCTOR TEAMWORK

You and your physician or nurse-midwife form an inseparable team when it comes to developing strategies for the safest possible pregnancy and birth for you and your babies. The physician and nurse-midwife contribute professional expertise, but you know your body better than they do. Also, these are your babies and you will be responsible for their care during the next 20-plus years, and some of these pregnancy decisions may affect caring for them once they have arrived.

The impact of pregnancy and birth lasts a lifetime. You, the person most affected by these events, and your partner, who is also concerned about the babies, should decide on the degree of involvement you will each have in any decision-making.

Self-care Participation

How can you participate in health-care decisions about your pregnancy if you don't have a health-care background? There are many things anyone can do:

1. Choose an obstetrical care provider who respects your role in decision-making and one with expertise in multiple pregnancy.
2. Examine your personal needs and goals for this experience.
3. Read about multiple pregnancy and birth.
4. Ask health-care providers questions related to the experience.

Choosing "expert" health care. A multiple pregnancy is not the same as a single-infant pregnancy, so you may have to determine whether your "regular" obstetrician-gynecologist or nurse-midwife is the best choice to work with you during a multiple pregnancy and birth. You are more likely to be referred to a specialist called a perinatologist if you are carrying higher-order multiples, but twin pregnancies are very different from single-infant pregnancies too. An obstetrician or nurse-midwife should be knowledgeable about the differences for multiple pregnancy and birth. Either should be prepared to explain those differences, and how they might treat them. However, an obstetrician or nurse-midwife also should evaluate and treat you and your multiple pregnancy as unique. All multiple pregnancies are not the same, and medical care should be individualized.

If you have been seeing a specialist in reproductive medicine, you've probably developed trust in that specialist. Yet women often must find a new physician once a pregnancy is achieved and they often say it takes time to transfer trust to a new health-care provider. You will feel more in control and better able to develop trust if you interview obstetricians and midwives to find one with expertise in multiple pregnancy and the willingness to support your personal goals for the pregnancy and birth.

Personal needs and goals. Multiple pregnancy and birth requires flexibility, because situations requiring medical intervention are more likely to arise. Still, gaining a better idea of your goals may offer some direction if choosing an obstetric care provider for a multiple pregnancy. It also provides a basis for becoming involved as an equal partner in working for the health of yourself and your babies.

Consider your answers to these or similar questions. How much do you want to be involved in, or in control of, your pregnancy and birth experience? When you think of birth, what is most important to you? (Take this question beyond the normal desire for healthy babies and think about the kind of birth experience you would like to have.) When you determine what you consider to be important, you will have an idea of your personal goals and an idea of the questions to ask obstetric care providers about their approaches to multiple pregnancy and birth. Questions might include:

- Does the care provider stick to a routine for all multiple pregnancies or does she/he take a flexible approach? What elements are considered crucial when monitoring a multiple pregnancy?
- What medical interventions are more likely to be recommended for multiple pregnancy, labor, and birth than for a single infant?
- What are the criteria for deciding whether multiples may be delivered vaginally versus cesarean? What is the provider's rate of vaginal versus cesarean twin births? Does the provider believe higher-order multiples can ever be delivered vaginally?
- Does multiple pregnancy change medication or anesthesia options for labor or birth? If yes, how do your options differ?
- How would the care provider recommend you best prepare for the various situations related to a twin or higher-order multiple pregnancy and birth? Does the obstetrician consider you as an equal member of the health-care team or are you expected to comply with recommendations for medical care no matter what?
- Does the obstetrician have delivery "privileges" at a hospital with a high level III NICU?

Once you have chosen an obstetric care provider, you may want to consider where to give birth.

- What options are available at the hospital where you will deliver? Will these options support your goals?
- Does the hospital have a policy regarding the management of multiple pregnancy and birth? If yes, what is it? Is the policy rigid or does it allow for flexibility?
- Is the hospital equipped for all idiosyncrasies associated with multiple births? For example, does the hospital neonatal intensive care unit (NICU) keep all premature and sick newborns, or must they transfer newborns in certain situations? How far is it to the best-equipped NICU? Under what circumstances would you or your babies be safer in a hospital prepared for all complications? What are your feelings about the possibility of separation from one or more of your babies if any had to be transferred?

A hospital with a *regional* or *level III* NICU provides the highest level of care to premature or very sick infants. If multiples are born in a hospital with a level I or level II NICU and the babies are very premature or extremely sick, they would have to be transferred to a regional center for more extensive care. To avoid the need for transport to a different hospital and to minimize mother-babies separation, a regional center usually is recommended for the births of higher-order multiples. It also may be the best choice for any set of twins born at, or before, 34-weeks gestation.

Many expectant parents of multiples develop *birth plans* for several different situations to cover the

1. full-term (or close to full term), vaginal birth of each baby;
2. planned cesarean/surgical delivery of all babies;
3. emergency vaginal or surgical birth of a second or third multiple;
4. premature birth;
5. birth of one or more sick newborns requiring care in a NICU; and
6. occurrence of a complication affecting you.

A cesarean/surgical delivery is usually planned for higher-order multiple births, but a birth plan that outlines your preferences may still be helpful.

Review birth plans with obstetric care providers. Make copies for your husband, your care provider(s), any other labor support person who will be with you, and your hospital labor chart.

Reading material. There are many books for parents expecting multiples. Some focus specifically on pregnancy and birth. The most helpful ones emphasize preventing complications commonly associated with multiple pregnancies, but they also focus on the early detection and treatment of such complications should any occur. Childbirth classes developed especially for parents expecting multiples complement reading material, and interactions with other couples and the instructor will help you prepare even better. For more information about reading materials or childbirth classes designed for multiple pregnancy and birth, see Appendix A: Suggested Reading, Appendix B: Resources—Childbirth Preparation Classes for Multiple Birth, and read Keys 3 and 4.

Asking questions. You can't ask too many questions during pregnancy about your health and that of your babies. Besides questions that refer to personal goals for the experience, ask about *any* recommended intervention or treatment. Ask questions that begin with "who," "what," "where," "when," "how," or "why," because a more detailed response is required.

You may not be able to make well-informed decisions about your health care during pregnancy and birth if you don't ask questions, such as, "Why do you recommend . . . ?" or "What scientific evidence is available that I . . . gain X number of pounds; eat this type of diet; go for serial ultrasounds; quit work early; initiate strict bed rest; take medications to prevent or halt preterm labor; monitor uterine contractions and let you regularly measure cervical length or check fetal fibrinectin; count fetal movements for an hour daily; or go for nonstress tests?"

Why ask "Why"? The key concept in health care today is "evidence-based care." This refers to using interventions and treatments that have been found helpful or effective with research testing. Expectant parents should be told whether a treatment has been shown to be effective or whether it is little more than a good guess that it will be of help. You also should be made aware of potential side effects in advance.

Many of the interventions and treatments commonly recommended during multiple pregnancy have little research support, and some have deleterious side effects. Different care providers may define certain terms or treatments differently. As the one most affected by any intervention or treatment, you should be informed of potential risks as well as potential benefits, and then make decisions about treatments with your obstetric care providers. (For a more detailed discussion of interventions, see Key 7.)

Doctors and midwives who are confident of their knowledge and abilities welcome questions. These obstetric care providers understand that it is not only your right, it also is your responsibility to care for yourself and your unborn babies. They know that you are more likely to follow a treatment regimen when you understand the reasons behind it. If an obstetric care provider seems unwilling or is unable to answer questions or explain the reasoning behind any recommendations or if you become uncomfortable with the care you are receiving, it is your prerogative to get a second opinion or change care providers.

Other Concerns

Let your obstetric care providers know how you feel about having multiples. Share any fears you might have about the pregnancy or the babies' birth, and tell them if you have any concerns about taking two or more newborns home. You should be able to depend on your obstetric care provider for information about organizations for parents of multiples and other parent groups, additional written materials, and referral to other health professionals who might be helpful, such as dietitians, lactation consultants, labor and postpartum doulas, and mental health counselors.

The Final Analysis

Not everyone wants the same thing from multiple pregnancy and birth. You may choose an active decision-making role or you may prefer to take a back seat and trust your care providers without question. No one can tell you how to feel or how involved to be. However, it is vitally important that you, as your babies' parents, and your health-care provider feel comfortable within this relationship. If you are satisfied with the way your obstetric care providers handle routine questions and situations, you probably will trust their judgments if an unexpected situation arises.

It takes teamwork to achieve the healthiest outcome for you and all your babies. Neither you nor the health-care provider can do it alone. The obstetrician or midwife needs your input to tailor health care to you and your babies' needs. Their expertise is only as good as your willingness to follow a treatment plan. Expect to receive the best health care for your unique situation only if you take the time to analyze your feelings and then ask questions that will help you understand any medical recommendations.

3

RISK FACTORS

Multiple pregnancy is automatically labeled as a "high risk" pregnancy. Being considered high risk means that the potential is higher for developing certain pregnancy and birth complications than for a woman having a single baby. It does not mean that you or your babies definitely will experience a complication.

Common Infant Complications

The most common complications for infants in multiple pregnancy are *low birth weight* (LBW) associated with *preterm* (premature) labor and birth or *intrauterine growth restriction* (IUGR), which also may be referred to as *fetal growth restriction* (FGR), or a combination of preterm birth *and* growth restriction. LBW is defined as any infant birth weight of less than 5 pounds, 8 ounces (2,500 g). An infant is considered to be *very low birth weight* (VLBW), which is also termed *extremely low birth weight* (ELBW), when the birth weight is 3 pounds, 3 ounces (1,500 g) or less.

LBW is important because these infants are more likely to experience physical distress during labor and after birth, so they are more likely to require care in a neonatal intensive care unit (NICU). LBW and VLBW babies are more at risk for several physical conditions, particularly certain respiratory conditions, during their entire first year. Developmental delays are seen more often among LBW infants. Certain neurologic impairments, such as cerebral palsy are more common for infants who were VLBW.

Of single infants, approximately 6 percent are LBW and only 1 percent are VLBW. Yet over half of twins are affected by low birth weight and 10 percent are VLBW. More than 90 percent of triplets are LBW, and of these triplets, more than 30 percent can be classified as VLBW. For each additional infant in a set of higher-order multiples, the number of LBW and VLBW infants increases.

Preterm labor. Pregnancy is also called the period of *gestation*, and you may hear either term used. A normal pregnancy lasts 38 to 42 weeks, and the average length of gestation for a single-infant pregnancy is between 39 and 39½ weeks. However, the average length of gestation is about three weeks less for each multiple a woman carries. This results in pregnancies of about 36 weeks for twins, 33 weeks for triplets, and 30 to 31 weeks for quadruplets and quintuplets.

Any baby that is born before 37 weeks gestation is considered *preterm* and a baby born before 33 weeks gestation may be called *very preterm.* More than 50 percent of twins and over 90 percent of triplets are born before 37 weeks compared with fewer than 10 percent of single-born infants born before 37 weeks. Less than 2 percent of single infants are very preterm, yet almost 14 percent of twins and more than 40 percent of triplets fall into that category. Preterm birth is associated with the immaturity of an infant's body and physical systems. The low birth weight of preterm infants is a reflection of this immaturity.

Intrauterine/fetal growth restriction. The average range in weight for a fetus or newborn is known for each week of gestation. When a newborn's birth weight is below the tenth percentile for gestational age, whether that newborn is full term or preterm, the baby is considered *small for gestational age* (SGA). The growth of a SGA baby is restricted in some way during development in the mother's uterus.

A little more than 9 percent of newborn singletons are SGA at birth, whereas more than 35 percent of twins and over 90 percent of triplets are SGA even when they are born after 37 weeks. Twins and single infants follow a similar growth curve until about 30 weeks gestation, at which time twin sets' rate of growth begins to decline. A decrease in growth rate is noted a week or two earlier for each additional fetus a woman carries.

Often the degree of growth restriction is quite different between or among the multiple fetuses, and it is said the babies' growth is *discordant*. When multiples have individual placentas, one placenta may develop more fully than another so that a certain fetus has more access to nutrients to help her grow. Connections between blood vessels can occur when monozygotic (MZ) (identical) twins share a single placenta. These vascular connections may result in a disproportionate amount of the fetal blood, which circulates in the placenta, to reach one twin. This condition is called *twin-to-twin transfusion syndrome* (TTTS). The (donor) twin receives less blood and becomes anemic and growth restricted; the (recipient) twin receives more and becomes larger. The consequences from these vessel-to-vessel connections vary depending on the type of blood vessels involved and the degree to which transfusion occurs. A severe form of TTTS is seen in about 1 to 2 percent of the 75 percent of MZ twin sets who share one placenta, and it is life-threatening for both twins.

Common Maternal Complications

Pregnancy-induced hypertension (PIH). PIH, often referred to as preeclampsia or toxemia of pregnancy, is the most common complication for women experiencing a multiple pregnancy. This condition is two to three times more likely to develop during multiple pregnancy. The cause of this condition is not well understood, but it generally is characterized by several physical changes in an expectant mother. These changes include a sharp increase in the woman's blood pressure, the "spilling" of protein in her urine, and a sudden, large gain in weight due to severe fluid retention. However, PIH in multiple pregnancy does not always follow the typical course, and the warning signs may differ. (See Key 5.)

Anemia. Iron-deficiency anemia is fairly common during multiple pregnancy, yet it is associated with increased risks for both a woman and her babies. PIH, infection, and postpartum hemorrhage occur more frequently among anemic women. Babies are more likely to be affected by preterm birth, growth restriction, and low birth weight if their mother was anemic during pregnancy.

Postpartum hemorrhage. Excessive bleeding or actual hemorrhage after delivery is more common with multiples and may be related to several factors or a combination of factors. A uterus that is overenlarged or overdistended from the size and weight of two or more infants may have difficulty contracting strongly after the birth. One large or two (or more) placentas took a larger area of uterine space, so there is a larger area to bleed from as most postpartum bleeding occurs at placental implantation sites. When hemorrhage occurs, it often is due to bleeding from a larger area in combination with a poorly contracting uterus. However, medications often used during multiple pregnancy or birth, such as magnesium sulfate for preterm labor or PIH or oxytocin to induce or augment labor may contribute to the conditions associated with hemorrhage. Mothers of multiples should be watched closely throughout their hospital stay for signs of hemorrhage.

The Risks Realistically

Although complications occur more often in multiple pregnancy, it is possible to avoid some problems and minimize others during a twin pregnancy. Many women have healthy, uncomplicated twin pregnancies. Concentrate on being among the 55 percent that give birth at or after 37 weeks or the almost 50 percent that have babies with birth weights above 5 pounds, 8 ounces (2,500 g). Who knows? After months of hearing that you should expect to give birth early, you may discover you are among the 14 percent to reach full-term gestation or the almost 20 percent to have a baby weighing more than 6 pounds, 11 ounces (3,000 g).

Fewer higher-order multiple pregnancies will completely avoid complications. Still, there are actions a woman can take that may decrease the incidence of some complications and lessen the effects of others. For a discussion of decreasing risk in all multiple pregnancies, see Key 4.

4

DECREASING THE
RISKS

WHAT CAN MOTHERS DO?

Risks associated with multiple pregnancy are less for a woman who is a well-nourished nonsmoker in good general health at the time of conception. If you've experienced a prior full-term pregnancy, the risk is lesser still. Prepregnancy health provides clues about your body's ability to adapt to the added stress of multiple fetuses. Good cardiovascular function is especially important, as your cardiovascular system is essential in the development and maintenance of one large or two (or more) placenta(s).

A placenta is the most short-lived yet most amazing organ of the human body. During pregnancy it constantly provides multiples with the oxygen and nutrients each requires for growth and development while it eliminates waste through the mother's circulation. It also produces hormones that help maintain the pregnancy.

The physical changes of pregnancy that support placental function are greater during a multiple pregnancy. In addition to covering a larger area of the uterus, the greater amount of fluid (plasma) that develops and circulates through a woman's blood vessels (expanded blood volume) and increased nutritional reserves also contribute to the health of the placenta(s).

What's a Mother to Do?
Maternal diet appears to play an important role in helping each placenta stay healthy, so the most important thing you can do is to eat enough for the three, four, five, or more of you. When living in a culture where "thin is in," it is easy to confuse the

changes of multiple pregnancy with getting fat. You may have to remind yourself frequently that you are not getting fat; you are growing two, three, or more healthy babies!

There are many aspects of multiple pregnancy that are beyond your control, but you can control what and how much you eat. It takes a lot of nutritious food to support the physical changes of pregnancy and the development of two or more growing babies.

Foods from all the food groups, which includes fats, should be part of daily meals and snacks. Supplementary vitamins and minerals, such as iron, are usually prescribed for any pregnancy, but they may be especially important during a multiple pregnancy.

Just as the physical changes of multiple pregnancy tend to be exaggerated, anything a woman puts in her mouth can have an exaggerated *positive* or *negative* effect on the babies' health and their placenta(s). This includes nonfood items, such as nutritional supplements, high-dose vitamin or mineral supplements, herbal supplements, tobacco, caffeine, alcohol, and all medications— whether prescription, over-the-counter, or "street" drugs.

- *Medications* that have little effect on a nonpregnant body may create dangerous side effects for a woman or her babies during pregnancy. Ask your obstetric care provider or a pharmacist before taking any medication.
- Women may be advised to take *higher doses* of certain *vitamins or minerals* during a multiple pregnancy. However, the benefits or risks of taking any such supplements should first be discussed with the obstetric care provider or a dietitian. Not all types or doses are safe.
- *Smoking* has long been associated with a higher incidence of preterm labor and birth, placental problems, PIH, and other complications. Studies show the dangers of tobacco use increase during multiple pregnancy.

Weight gain. Weight gain is one indicator of how well your body is adapting to multiple pregnancy. Increased weight gain has been associated with longer length of gestation and higher birth weights for all multiple pregnancies.

17

A gain of at least 40 to 45 pounds (18–20.5 kg) is recommended for a twin pregnancy. Gains of more than 45 to 50 pounds (20.5–23 kg) are common among women having full-term twin pregnancies and giving birth to two babies with birth weights of more than 5 pounds, 8 ounces (2,500 g) each.

For triplet pregnancies, weight gains of more than 50 pounds (23 kg) are associated with increased length of gestation and bigger babies. Those pregnant with quadruplets or more should work to gain at least 50 pounds, plus an extra 5 pounds (2.25 kg) for each additional fetus.

A weekly gain of approximately 1 pound (0.5 kg) for the first 20 to 24 weeks of a twin pregnancy and 1.5 pounds (0.7 kg) for the remaining weeks is encouraged. The average gain per week increases for triplet and quadruplet pregnancies. Some women gain a steady amount of weight from week to week or month to month. Others find they gain in spurts with smaller than average gains one week (or month) and larger than average gains during others.

Nausea and possibly vomiting (morning sickness) during the first several months of pregnancy often is more severe during multiple pregnancy, resulting in no gain or an initial weight loss. Some women seem to make up for this loss by gaining more than average amounts once nausea subsides.

Multiple pregnancy is *not* the time to diet or limit weight gain. A larger than usual weight gain (1.5 pounds, or 0.7 kg/week) may be completely healthy as long as your blood pressure is within normal limits, you experience no sudden body swelling, and urine does not contain a significant amount of protein. Still, you may be monitored more closely if weight gain is significantly below or above current recommendations.

Postpartum weight loss is less likely to become an issue if your diet consisted of *nutritious* foods during your pregnancy. Eat foods in as close to their natural state as possible to avoid empty calories, unnecessary additives, and high levels of hidden salt.

However, a salt-free diet is not desirable. Some salt may be necessary for a healthy multiple pregnancy.

A severe form of nausea and vomiting, called *hyperemesis gravidarum*, is more common during multiple pregnancy. Yet eating and early weight gain are important. Many women eat starchy foods, such as crackers or bread, before they get out of bed in the morning. Blander foods may suit your stomach better until nausea subsides. Eating small, frequent meals often minimizes nausea or stomach upset early in pregnancy. Severe nausea or hyperemesis gravidarum may require medical treatment, so let your obstetric care provider know if you have difficulty keeping food or liquid down.

As pregnancy progresses, multiples take up a lot of room, so your stomach has less space. Eating several small meals rather than three large ones each day often helps. Experts also recommend snacking every one to two hours.

Some women find high-protein, liquid supplements provide nutrients they need yet are easier on their stomachs during later pregnancy. But discuss it first with the obstetric care provider or a dietitian. Some may be inappropriate during multiple pregnancy.

Fluid. There is a lot of extra fluid in circulation during multiple pregnancy, so you may be thirstier. Blood volume expansion is normal to help meet the demands of the expectant mother's body, the growing fetuses, and the placenta(s) that nourish them. However, compare the 50 percent increase in blood volume for a single-infant pregnancy with the 75 percent increase of a twin pregnancy or the almost 90 to 95 percent increase when carrying higher multiples! That's a lot of extra liquid!

Don't ignore thirst. Drink 100-percent-fruit juices, milk, or water whenever you eat a snack or a meal. If you're ever concerned about hydration, check your urine. It should be a pale, straw yellow color. Simply drink more fluid if urine looks darker.

Dehydration may be associated with preterm labor, a common complication of multiple pregnancy, and *strict bed rest* is often recommended after an episode of preterm labor. Surprisingly, a woman may need to *drink more* fluid rather than less when on bed rest, because it affects secretion of the antidiuretic hormone (ADH), which helps maintain adequate fluid in body tissues. During strict bed rest, large amounts of fluid may be lost through urination and sweating. (See Key 8 for a discussion of bed rest.)

Vitamins and minerals. Extra iron and folic acid may be prescribed because anemia occurs more often during multiple pregnancy. Although it is beneficial to eat iron-rich foods, tremendous quantities of those foods must be eaten to get enough extra iron during multiple pregnancy. Iron supplements sometimes cause nausea or constipation, so you might ask about a timed-release form if extra iron is prescribed.

Dietitian consult. Centers providing care for high-risk pregnancies often have a *registered* or *licensed dietitian* (RD and/or LD) specializing in perinatal nutrition on the staff. A consult early in pregnancy may provide pregnancy-risk-reducing ideas. The guidance of a dietitian may be especially helpful if you

1. smoke in any amount
2. were underweight or significantly overweight at conception
3. have a history of an eating disorder
4. are on a special diet, such as vegetarian
5. are carrying higher-order multiples.

Also consult a perinatal dietitian if you ever have difficulty gaining adequate weight or if you are coping with any health condition or pregnancy complication that affects nutrition, such as heart or kidney conditions and any type of diabetes. Strict bed rest can suppress appetite and affects body fluid balance, so talk to a dietitian about maintaining weight gain if it's advised. (To locate a perinatal dietitian, see Appendix B: Resources, Perinatal Dietitians.)

My Diet Is Perfect, but . . .

No matter how well a woman eats during multiple pregnancy, a complication may occur. Many of the factors contributing to complications are beyond anyone's control and many are unpredictable. Still, you and your babies are more likely to do well, in spite of any complication, if you have been eating well and gaining adequate weight during multiple pregnancy.

5

〰〰〰〰〰〰〰〰〰〰〰〰〰〰〰〰〰〰〰〰〰〰〰〰〰〰〰

WHAT TO KNOW—JUST IN CASE

Obstetric care providers follow multiple pregnancies closely, but the expectant mother knows her own body best. You can help care providers tremendously by becoming aware of the signs that signal the most common complications.

Preterm labor. To give babies more time to grow, get to *know your uterus.* Ask your obstetric care provider to help you find its outline. Become familiar with its usual "feel" so you will know the difference during a uterine contraction, when it will tighten or "ball" up and be difficult to push in on. Although you may have occasional painless contractions, pay attention to changes in how loose or tight your uterus feels during different levels of activity. Note how often any contractions occur. By becoming sensitive to the feel of your uterus, you will be alert for any unusual change.

The preterm birth of multiples can sometimes be avoided or delayed if a mother recognizes the signs of preterm labor and takes appropriate action. If you ever suspect preterm labor, do *not* wait to see if symptoms stop. *Lie down, drink extra fluid,* and *call your obstetric care provider* IMMEDIATELY if you experience even *one* of these symptoms:

- Four uterine contractions (even if painless) within one hour
- Intermittent or continuous pelvic pressure
- Intermittent or continuous low backache or cramping, such as menstrual-type cramping
- Any increase in vaginal discharge, including mucous, blood, or water

Fetal growth and development. You can help monitor the babies' well-being by counting their movements every day during the last trimester. From the 28th week of pregnancy with twins or the 24th week with higher-order multiples, take a *kick count* during the same one-hour rest break each day. Some expectant mothers can differentiate the movements of each baby, but others find it impossible to tell. Take the daily kick count regardless of who you think is where!

Have a pen and paper handy to mark down each time you feel even the slightest fetal movement. Count the total number of movements. A count of five movements per baby (10 for twins, 15 for triplets, and so on) per hour is about average. Don't be alarmed if there are fewer than average movements. You may have chosen a period of less activity or the babies may be sleeping. Try counting at a different time of day, or become aware of day-to-day pattern if the most convenient time to count is when babies are resting.

You may notice less movement as babies get closer to term and the uterus becomes more crowded. Still, call the obstetric care provider any time a *significant* decrease or increase in any baby's activity is noticed.

Maternal pregnancy-induced hypertension (PIH). Women develop PIH more often and symptoms can arise more abruptly or progress more quickly during multiple pregnancy. Since this condition affects both mother and babies, early detection is important to minimize the consequences. It is crucial to keep all prenatal health care appointments so that blood pressure, weight gain and urine can be closely monitored. Report *any* rapid body swelling (edema), upper abdominal pain, severe headache, spots floating in front of the eyes, and blurred or decreased vision to the obstetric provider IMMEDIATELY.

A more severe form of PIH known as HELLP syndrome occurs more often in multiple pregnancy. The acronym stands for hemolysis (intravascular) [H], elevated liver (enzymes) [EL], and low platelets [LP]. If a woman is affected by PIH during multiple pregnancy, obstetric care providers will closely monitor for any signs of HELLP syndrome so they can intervene right away. An intervention that is sometimes necessary is the preterm delivery of the multiples.

Researchers recently reported less PIH in "at risk" women when they took supplements of specific vitamins and minerals as part of their diets. You may want to ask your obstetric care provider about this research. Do *not* add higher than usual doses of any vitamins or minerals, however, without first discussing it with the provider.

"Can't hurt but not sure if they help" Interventions

In addition to eating well and gaining enough weight, several other interventions may be suggested to decrease risks associated with multiple pregnancy.

Rest and exercise. Many care providers recommend taking several 30- to 60-minute daily rest breaks, with feet propped or lying toward one side, by the 20th to 24th week of a twin pregnancy. Because of the increased risk of preterm labor, be prepared to begin a leave of absence from employment and to get help with heavier household chores *at least* by the 30th week of pregnancy (or earlier).

Most obstetric care providers encourage women to engage in mild exercise and "activities of living" during twin pregnancy, unless some sign of preterm labor is detected. However, vigorous exercise, the kind that causes one to "break a sweat," may be discouraged because excessive activity is associated with increased uterine contractions.

When pregnant with higher-order multiples, activity may be limited to performing only simple activities of daily living by the 20th to 24th week (or earlier). Expect to be placed under "house arrest" and taking frequent rest breaks by this time, which means it will be necessary to take an earlier leave of absence from one's place of employment.

Intimate activity restrictions. Oxytocin and prostaglandins are hormones associated with uterine contractions. Because of the increased incidence of preterm labor, some obstetric providers suggest women avoid unnecessary exposure to these hormones during multiple pregnancy. A halt to sexual activity involving nipple stimulation or resulting in female orgasm may be recommended, since oxytocin is released during either. To avoid cervical exposure to prostaglandins, providers may recommend using a condom during intercourse, since male semen contains prostaglandin. Other forms of physical intimacy usually are acceptable, but ask the provider if there is any question.

Breastfeeding. Oxytocin also triggers the milk-ejection reflex (let-down) during breastfeeding. If a woman is breastfeeding a child when multiple pregnancy is discovered, weaning is likely to be recommended. Whether slow or an abrupt weaning is necessary may depend on level of risk of preterm labor for a specific multiple pregnancy.

Alternative techniques. Relaxation techniques may prolong some pregnancies at risk for preterm labor and birth. Among the techniques studied are body massage, progressive muscle relaxation, guided imagery, hypnosis or self-hypnosis, biofeedback, and therapeutic touch. Some relaxation interventions can be accomplished alone or with your partner, and rest breaks may offer the perfect opportunity for practice. Others require the help of a trained therapist.

You Do Make a Difference

You can decrease the possibility of multiple pregnancy complications by becoming well informed and involved in prenatal care. You don't have to "just wait and see." Your participation in your care does make a healthy difference. (See Keys 3, 6, and 7.)

6

~~~~~~

DECREASING THE RISKS

WHAT CAN OBSTETRIC CARE PROVIDERS DO?

A healthy mother and healthy babies is the pregnancy outcome desired by all obstetric care providers. Because multiple pregnancies are at greater risk for complications, they usually are monitored more closely. Frequent prenatal care visits and certain prenatal tests are recommended more often. This close surveillance serves to reassure when all is going well, detect a complication early to minimize possible consequences, and keep a closer eye on babies and mother should a complication occur.

Screening tools can produce valuable information about the health and well-being of an expectant mother and her babies, and their use helps guide health-care treatment during multiple pregnancy. Still, most screening tools offer only inexact information. Expectant parents should learn about screening tools so they can weigh the benefits and risks of using any that may be recommended for their multiple pregnancy. They also will be able to ask about possible use if the health provider doesn't mention it first.

Discovering Multiples

Laboratory test values often provide the first clue that a woman is carrying more than one baby. The values obtained for the lab tests commonly done during the first 20 weeks of pregnancy are all higher with multiple pregnancy. These tests may include maternal serum human chorionic gonadotropin (hCG) (pregnancy test kits) and alpha-fetoprotein (AFP). Human placental lactogen (HPL) also is higher. (The letters "MS" for "maternal serum" may be included as part of a test name abbreviation, such as MSAFP.) Once lab results provide the clue, ultrasound is usually ordered.

Ultrasound has made it possible to detect a multiple pregnancy within weeks of conception, and many multiples are discovered using this tool. An early sonogram is considered routine when conception occurs with the help of ovulatory-induction medications or assisted reproductive techniques. Early ultrasound has led to the discovery that a *vanishing twin*, when one (or more) embryo stops developing and disappears from subsequent sonograms, is a fairly common phenomenon, although knowledge of its occurrence does not lessen the grief many women feel when an embryo stops developing. As multiple pregnancy progresses, ultrasound becomes a window to the womb, allowing obstetric care providers to keep an eye on the little ones growing within.

Routine Screening Procedures

Obstetric care providers derive a wealth of crucial health information during routine prenatal visits. Many women are unaware of how much is learned from frequent observation, weight checks, urine specimens, blood pressure readings, fetal heart tone counts, palpation of uterine size, and so on. Obstetric providers may want to see women with multiple pregnancies more often from the 12th week of a higher-order pregnancy or from the 24th week of a twin pregnancy.

Preterm Labor

Preterm labor and birth are the most common complications of multiple pregnancy, and their prevention is a main focus of obstetric care. In addition to being alert for symptoms of preterm labor, the obstetric care provider may monitor for other early physical signs. Several different kinds of screening tools *may* be used, but use varies among obstetric providers and in different areas or countries.

- The lower portion of the uterus, also called the cervix, softens, thins out, and dilates during labor to allow a baby's passage into the birth canal (vagina). Many providers recommend frequent *evaluation* by manual exam or transvaginal ultrasound to monitor cervical length and dilation.

- *Fetal fibronectin* (fFn) is a protein that helps the chorion adhere to the uterus—sort of like a glue. It is normally found in vaginal secretions up to the 22nd week of pregnancy, but secretions should be negative for fFn between 22 and 36 weeks. When a vaginal swab is negative for fFn, preterm labor is highly unlikely for at least two weeks. Detection of fFn in the secretions *does not* mean preterm labor will definitely occur, but its presence alerts a woman and the obstetric providers to pay closer attention for symptoms of preterm labor.

Fetal Surveillance

When obstetric providers monitor the babies' health and well-being it is referred to as *fetal surveillance*. During multiple pregnancy, providers check on the individual fetuses and also consider each in comparison to the others. The following screening tools may be used to keep an eye on multiple babies, but their use varies depending on providers' clinical findings and an individual situation.

- Salivary *estriol* testing looks for a hormonal marker, which at certain levels reassures providers that babies are doing well. As with fFn, a less reassuring number only alerts providers to watch more closely, and a multiple pregnancy can actually "confuse" results.
- *Ultrasound,* or sonograms, may be ordered to check for the number of amnions or for placental vascular connections when twins appear to be monochorionic monozygotes. (See Key 1.) Obtaining an *amniotic fluid index* (AFI) via ultrasound can help providers measure and compare the amount of amniotic fluid in each baby's amniotic sac, which may be of value in suspected or diagnosed twin-to-twin transfusion syndrome (TTTS) and fetal growth restriction.
- As pregnancy progresses, serial ultrasound may be used to monitor babies' individual growth patterns and to compare babies' sizes. Babies' activity and breathing movements may be examined alone or in conjunction with a nonstress test (NST) to cre-

ate a *biophysical profile* (BPP). An ultrasound test may be ordered for *placental grading* to check for calcifications associated with placenta "aging." A *doppler flow study*, sometimes referred to as umbilical cord velocimetry, may be ordered to observe blood flow in the babies' umbilical cords.

* A *nonstress test* (NST) measures the response of each fetus's heart rate to fetal movement through the use of external electronic fetal monitor (EFM) equipment. Their responses, or reactivity, provide clues about the fetuses' well-being. Fetal heart rate is detected through an ultrasound device attached to an elastic belt the expectant mother wears. One belt per multiple is needed to monitor more than one at once. NST may be ordered with preterm labor, term pregnancy, signs of growth restriction in one or more fetuses, placental grading, and so on.

Part of the Team

Close monitoring helps obstetric care providers gain the information needed to avoid or keep multiple pregnancy risks to a minimum. With early detection of a complication, intervention or treatment can begin sooner. Still, science has a lot to learn about multiple pregnancies, so expectant parents should be aware of and ask lots of questions about any recommended screening procedure.

7

MEDICAL INTERVENTION

Medical intervention can take different forms during multiple pregnancy. Sometimes an intervention is suggested with the hope of completely preventing a potential pregnancy complication. A nutritious diet and adequate weight gain are examples of interventions that can help prevent preterm labor, fetal growth restriction, and PIH. Other interventions or treatments may be recommended or introduced only after screening tests or symptoms indicate the possibility of a complication.

Medical science has learned a great deal about multiple pregnancy in recent decades, but it has a long way to go before the "best" way to routinely manage multiple pregnancies is developed. Many suggested treatments or interventions are not supported by evidence that they actually work. Thus, parents must be ready to discuss the potential benefits and risks of common interventions.

Controversial Treatment

Certain interventions may be very beneficial and quite appropriate if symptoms of particular complications occur. Controversy arises, however, when there is no research evidence that the same intervention actually prevents a certain complication during multiple pregnancies, yet that intervention carries the possibility of serious side effects for a mother or her babies. Intervention should be implemented only when the potential consequences of a particular complication create more risk for babies or mother than the potential effects of the planned intervention.

Interventions that may be helpful for certain situations but are considered controversial if recommended routinely or before symptoms occur include:

- strict bed rest regimens
- tocolytic use—medication to inhibit uterine contractions
- cervical cerclage—suturing procedure to hold the cervix closed
- corticosteroids—medication to "speed" fetal lung development.

Bed rest. Recommendations to decrease activity, eliminate vigorous exercise, add frequent rest periods, or begin "house arrest" with an early leave of absence may be appropriate even during a healthy *twin pregnancy*, because of increased uterine irritability. Strict bed rest has not been found to prevent preterm labor. Although some believe it decreases pressure on the cervix or "saves" an expectant mother's energy, bed rest does not appear to improve twin pregnancy outcomes.

The research on prolonged, strict bed rest during *higher-order multiple pregnancy* is inconclusive. Although the number of these pregnancies has increased, they still occur infrequently, so it is difficult to compare "routine" strict bed rest regimens with less stringent ones.

Strict bed rest, in which a woman is not to get up at all or only to go to the bathroom, has been associated with profound physiologic change affecting every system in the body. Weight loss often occurs because appetite is suppressed and fluid is lost through increased sweating and urination. The body metabolizes steroids and sugar (glucose) differently. Thyroid function is affected. Muscle atrophy (shrinking) and deconditioning of the cardiovascular system begins within days and, if prolonged, can take months to recondition after delivery. Depression is common for both expectant parents, especially when strict bed rest is prolonged.

Strict bed rest may be the only available option if significant cervical change occurs (with or without signs of preterm labor) during a twin pregnancy or for higher-order pregnancies, but it should never be recommended casually or routinely. Be sure the obstetric provider clearly defines "bed rest" if it is recommended. The term does not mean the same thing to all care providers.

When strict bed rest is unavoidable, an expectant mother should be referred to a perinatal dietitian to improve her nutritional status and to counteract potential weight loss and fluid depletion. Physical therapy to maintain maternal muscle strength and cardiac conditioning may be beneficial. Counseling to help an expectant couple cope with the psychological effects also should be considered. (See Appendix B: Resources—Bed Rest.)

Tocolytics. A tocolytic is a medication that has been found to halt or decrease uterine contractions. These medications can play an important role in prolonging multiple pregnancy if preterm labor occurs, but there is no evidence that tocolytic use prevents the onset of preterm labor. Women taking tocolytics during multiple pregnancy are at somewhat higher risk for developing severe cardiopulmonary (heart and lungs) and circulatory system side effects. Close supervision of the woman and her babies is advised when using these medications.

Cervical cerclage. A cerclage is a surgical procedure in which sutures or a band are inserted in the cervix to prevent or limit cervical dilation in women having a history of recurrent pregnancy loss or preterm delivery due to *incompetent cervix*—a painless dilation of the cervix. It also may be recommended if significant cervical changes are noted before 24 weeks of pregnancy. However, inserting a cerclage during multiple pregnancy to prevent premature dilation of the cervix has *not* been found helpful; it is associated with an increased risk for cervical infection and maternal fever, which may contribute to preterm labor.

Corticosteroids. The health of preterm babies has greatly improved since it was discovered that giving a mother corticosteroids during preterm labor "speeds" fetal lung development. (You may hear the medication referred to as betamethasone, dexamethasone, or celestone.) This has resulted in fewer, or less severe, cases of respiratory distress syndrome (RDS) for preterm babies. Although the injection may be beneficial regardless of the time given before delivery, the steroids work best when preterm birth

31

can be delayed for 24 hours. The effect lasts about seven days, so repeated injections are given for later episodes of preterm labor.

Experts recommend administering steroids if preterm delivery is likely within seven days or if a complication may force providers to deliver babies prematurely within seven days. Otherwise, repeated or routine administration is not recommended; it can have negative effects on the expectant mother's immune status and is associated with side effects on babies. In higher-order multiple pregnancies, steroid use sometimes increases uterine contractions, so close supervision of uterine activity is important.

Multifetal reduction. Every risk associated with multiple pregnancy is heightened when a woman is carrying higher-order multiples. An option often suggested by obstetric providers early in a higher-order multiple pregnancy is multifetal reduction, a procedure that decreases the number of fetuses in the hope of decreasing the level of risk for the remaining babies and their mother. It can be a difficult option to consider after working so hard to get pregnant, and making a decision may cast a heavy shadow on what should be a joyous time. Not surprisingly, this option has created a moral and ethical dilemma for parents and obstetric care providers who must weigh the increased risks of multiple pregnancy for babies and mother with the life of one, two, and possibly all babies.

In the case of triplet pregnancy, most research indicates that outcomes are no better for the remaining babies after reducing a pregnancy from three to two, than for triplet pregnancies that are not reduced. Reduction does appear to improve outcomes when four or more fetuses are conceived. Expectant parents should also be aware that multifetal reduction is associated with a fairly high risk for loss of all the fetuses in a multiple pregnancy.

Working Together
The role of obstetric care providers in helping to minimize the risk of complications is especially important during multiple pregnancy. Expectant parents play an equally crucial role. Everyone must work together and weigh options that will result in the best outcome —a healthy mother and healthy multiple newborns.

8

‸‸‸

CHOOSING PEDIATRIC CARE

Shop for a supportive pediatrician, family physician, or pediatric nurse practitioner before your babies' expected arrival. You will spend a lot of time and money at a pediatric care provider's office in the next few years, so you need to find someone with whom you feel comfortable and confident. Choosing someone with a reassuring personality and a compatible child care philosophy is as important as ensuring that your babies' health-care provider has the appropriate credentials. This Key shares ideas for finding someone well suited to both you and your babies' needs.

The obstetric care provider, friends with children, and members of a local Mothers of Multiples Club or La Leche League group are good starting points for pediatric care recommendations. Consider the convenience of the pediatric provider's office location as well. Keep in mind, however, that it is not a good idea to choose the babies' care provider based *only* on the convenient location of the office or another's recommendation.

Once you have your list of recommendations, check with the health-care insurance company to be sure the providers you plan to interview are on your plan. Study the guidelines for handling emergency situations. Do you have to call your primary care provider before you can take baby to an emergency room? Today there are numerous restrictions placed on the insured.

Begin to interview pediatric providers from four to six months of the pregnancy, because of the greater possibility of preterm delivery. Many pediatric providers encourage a prenatal parent visit, some may prefer to talk with expectant parents over the telephone, and others ask one of their staff to handle these interviews. A pediatric provider's attitude about meeting or talking with parents early tells you a great deal about her/his approach.

If the pediatric practice includes a certified pediatric nurse practitioner (CPNP), consider interviewing her/him for well-baby care. A CPNP's service is generally less expensive than a physician's, and a CPNP often has more time for questions and concerns.

You may have more pediatric provider options if living in an urban area. This does not mean that there is no point in interviewing the only care provider available in a small rural town. You still learn a lot by talking with the health professional who will care for your babies before their arrival. Ask whether the practice has cared for many sets of multiples or preterm babies and if they have found any child-care issues to be of particular concern for parents of multiples. This may give you an idea of a provider's sensitivity to your unique situation.

Find out if anyone in the practice has a subspecialty, such as neonatology, developmental pediatrics, allergy, and so on. What hospitals are they affiliated with?

What special considerations will the practice make if your babies are preterm or any has an ongoing health problem? Will they make house calls or assure that multiples will be seen quickly to avoid exposure to sick children when you take them to the office, as preterm or compromised babies have less resistance to contagious illnesses, including Respiratory Syncytial Virus (RSV)?

Are the pediatric providers familiar with developmental and early intervention specialists and related programs in the area?

Ask if the pediatric practice offers a fee discount for more than one baby. Many pediatric providers recognize the financial strain that multiple well-baby visits place on a family. These providers may charge the full amount for each baby's immunizations and for the first baby's physical examination, but they deduct 50 to 100% from the other exams. Many practices also provide samples of medications, vitamins, or formula.

When breastfeeding, you will feel more confident if the pediatric professionals have a positive attitude about breastfeeding multiples. How many multiples in the practice have been breast-fed? What does the pediatric provider think about breastfeeding multiples? What attitude does the provider have about complementary or supplementary formula or starting solid foods? Does the practice employ or recommend a certified lactation consultant (IBCLC) or recommend contacting a breastfeeding support group, such as La Leche League or Nursing Mothers Association?

Visit the pediatrician's office. Check its physical arrangements. How easy would it be to take infants from the car to the office without another adult? Are there ramps and elevators that can accommodate a multiple stroller, or must you use stairs at some point? How many doors must you go through? Are they easy to open? Are the exam and waiting rooms childproofed?

Ask if the pediatric office has a separate waiting area for children suspected of having contagious diseases. Since you end up caring for multiple sick babies if even one contracts a communicable disease, you have more reason to avoid unnecessary illnesses!

Because you will be keeping track of more than one child in the waiting room, ask the receptionist which appointment time is best so your multiples can be seen more quickly. Usually the first appointments in the morning and after the lunch break are seen immediately. After those appointments the waiting area may back up.

Is there a special time when you can call to ask questions about the babies' growth or care? While getting to know two or more new babies, you are bound to have more questions and concerns than parents of a single infant. Some pediatric practices set aside a special hour or two for nonemergency calls, so parents do not have to worry that they are "bothering" the doctor.

No one pediatric provider is best for all babies or parents. If you are ever unhappy with your babies' health care for whatever reason, it is your prerogative to take them to another pediatric practice. By taking the time before the babies' birth to interview physicians, you are more likely to be satisfied.

9

~~~~~~

NAMING YOUR BABIES

N aming many babies, as with every other aspect of raising multiples, is more complicated than naming a single child. Give careful thought to the names you give your babies. A name separates a person from the masses and identifies someone as a unique individual. A multiple's name also sets him apart from the set.

Initially, it may sound like fun to name babies something matching—Ronnie, Donnie, and Connie (rhyming); Rose, Violet, and Daisy (flowers); Steve and Stephanie (male and female versions of the same name); John Adam, Jennifer Amelia, Jane Alice, Joyce Alisa (same initials); Alex and Andy (assonance); or Jennifer and Jessica (alliteration). Such names may encourage people to view multiples as a unit instead of as individuals. Is your goal to raise separate children who are proud to be a member of a set of multiples but not limited to it, or to reinforce the unit?

Interviews with adult twins indicate that some resent matching names but others do not mind. If your babies are not here yet, consider these factors.

- Rhyming names—Sharon, Karen, and Darren—may discourage individuality. They also lead to confusion since they sound so much alike. Just imagine the number of times in a lifetime you may hear, "Who?" or "I thought you wanted him, not me!"
- Friends, relatives, and teachers have difficulty remembering which name goes with which child, especially when names rhyme or have the same cadence. This happens even with fraternal multiples. One teacher complained that it took her months to remember which twin was Mandy and which was Wendy even though the girls barely looked like sisters.

- Giving boy/girl multiples the male/female version of a name—Stephen and Stephanie—encourages viewing them as a unit.
- Having the same initials as one's sibling confuses record keeping. One pharmacist altered one twin's birth date in his computer when the family insurance carrier kept refusing reimbursement for identical prescriptions, claiming duplicate forms were sent because the twins' initials were identical.
- If a father desperately wants a junior but has multiple-birth sons, consider the impact for the sons not named for their father.
- Cute baby "nicknames" may stay with children for a lifetime and may not be appreciated in adulthood.
- Giving multiples currently popular names may add yet another element to their identity issues.
- Be aware of other classifications of names as well. It may be better to stick to ethnic names (Omer and Katarina), trendy names (Tiffany, Cara, Chelsea, Maddie), unisex names (Taylor Baily, Casey, Jordan), and gender-specific names (Joseph and Catherine) for each.
- Naming babies after special people, such as grandparents, is a nice idea if you like all the names. This isn't the time to exclude someone, however. The child not named for a loved one will wonder why, and the grandparent left out may feel offended.
- Finally, while making your decision, say the names aloud. Do they sound "right" together? Do the names flow easily no matter which is said first? The same child may not want to be second, third, fourth, or fifth in rotation every time.

Everyone wants to know that her name was chosen especially for her and that it has some significance to her parents. You want your children to know that a lot of thought went into choosing their names.

10

BABY CARE PRODUCTS

If the thought of buying for multiples triggers panic, relax. Having multiples is more expensive than having one child, but it is not prudent or necessary to buy everything new or to double, triple, or quadruple all your purchases. Most Mothers of Multiples Clubs sponsor semiannual sales of well-maintained infant clothing and equipment. Consignment shops, garage sales, and church bazaars are other good sources.

Layette

The babies' layette does not have to be elaborate or coordinated. About 5 stretch sleepers or cotton gowns per baby and an equal number of T-shirts is enough for most newborns. Have several receiving blankets for each baby, and several crib sheets. Each baby needs a sweater and a hat, and a snowsuit for cold climates.

Diapers

Each baby will use as many diapers as any single baby. Each newborn will have to be changed approximately 100 times per week. If you use disposable diapers, the cost is doubled, tripled, or quadrupled, but they are convenient and available in sizes from premie through toddler. Sometimes a diaper service, pharmacy, online baby store, warehouse wholesaler, or grocery store will deliver disposable diapers.

You do not need to buy two, three, or more times the number of diapers if washing your own. You simply must wash them more often so washing diapers soon becomes part of the daily routine.

The more diapers you use, the more economical a diaper service becomes. The initial delivery charge does not change when there are more babies. The cost of additional diapers is usually minimal. Check with the services in your area, if available. A diaper service may be the least expensive option.

Car Seats

Car seats that meet federal guidelines for safety are a *must*. You may save money if you can purchase seats that serve babies from birth through the toddler years; however, an infant model may be a necessity for preterm multiples. Consider your car when choosing a particular model. Some do not work with certain seat belts, and others are so big that more than one or two will not fit in the car. For your babies' safety, be sure to install and use car seats according to the manufacturer's recommendation. Many police and fire departments offer car seat checks and instructions on the proper installation and use of car seats.

Cribs

Often two or three newborns can share a crib during their early months and maybe even later. Some sleep better when allowed to cosleep and cuddle. Between three and six months they may begin to disturb each other.

Any crib purchased or borrowed should meet current government guidelines for safety. At this time slats must be no more than 2⅜ inches apart because babies have strangled themselves when their heads slipped through (babies' heads may be small as a result of prematurity or low birth weight). Mattresses must fit snugly so babies' heads can't slip between the mattress and crib frame. Sheets should fit securely, so check them for shrinkage after each washing. Bumper pads should fit tightly but be removed as soon as babies can roll over or pull themselves up. Also, cribs should be free of projections that may catch on infants' clothing.

Stroller

Invest in a good double to quadruple stroller. Multiples use a stroller longer and more often than singletons because no parent has enough eyes or hands to manage more than one unconfined infant, toddler, or preschooler. The following is a list of the different types of strollers, with their advantages and disadvantages.

Some limousine-type strollers are heavy and long. Most are easy to push but require effort to get one in and out of a car. Either your twins face each other or both face forward.

Umbrella-type strollers are lightweight and inexpensive compared to other strollers. They are easy to handle when loading in and out of a car, but they often offer less support than other strollers, and many brands won't accommodate older children. Some become cumbersome or too heavy to push as babies grow.

There are lightweight imported strollers similar to traditional umbrella-type models that are sturdier; however, most are also more expensive. Yet at less than 36 inches wide, most double models will fit through doorways.

Tandem strollers have seats facing forward—one behind the other. The children in the back often have less legroom than the one in the front and they may not see as well from a back seat.

Midweight side-by-side double or triple strollers offer babies the same view but often won't fit through doorways.

There are double and triple sport strollers designed for athletic parents. These strollers are constructed so parents can jog while pushing two or three babies in comfort and safety. (Double and triple bicycle trailers are also available.)

Parents of higher-order multiples may have to order a stroller through a parents of multiples organization, a specialty store, or online. You'll have to decide what will work for you. Two double strollers may seem to be a more realistic option than one quadruple stroller, but this also means two adults must always be available to push them. You will not be able to go out by yourself unless you have a stroller that accommodates all at once.

Discuss the options with other mothers of multiples, but base the final decision on your family's needs and lifestyle. Be sure any stroller provides babies with good back support, and it should have a seatbelt for each and a good brake system. Check the return policy for special-ordered strollers or any purchased over the Internet, or you may have to keep an unwanted stroller. Also check the warranty for the frame and parts. You'll soon learn that multiples are harder on equipment than single children!

Soft Infant Carriers

There are some specially designed multiple-infant carriers. Few parents can safely carry more than two at once, but carriers still come in handy. A fussy baby who needs extra attention and mother contact can be placed in a carrier and kept close to mother's heart while she continues to care for the other babies.

Slings are adaptable soft carriers. Some parents place two babies in a single sling. Others crisscross two slings across the parent's body. (See Keys 33 and 35.)

Other Equipment

- Changing tables are nice, but they are not essential to perform the task. A clean towel, piece of flannel sheeting, or a changing pad on the floor, sofa, or bed will do just as well and allows for assembly-line diaper or clothing changes!
- Infant swings may keep babies pleasantly occupied while you feed another. If you have enough swings for each you may be able to sneak some time for your own meals. *However, never leave your babies unattended in swings!*
- Infant seats, especially those that bounce, are helpful. Babies can be bottle-fed while resting in infant seats. You can hold one baby for feeding, while gently bouncing another with a foot.
- A single play yard is generally too small to confine two or more active babies, but placing newborns in a play yard may protect them from older siblings. Later, these are wonderful for storing toys or keeping one child confined while tending to the other(s).

Nonessential Equipment

Jump-seats, bouncers, saucers, and other items are nonessential equipment. Walkers are associated with a high incidence of infant injury and visits to emergency rooms.

Buy only the essentials before the babies are born. Accept friends' equipment on loan. After they are here, you will gain a better idea of what equipment works best for you and your babies.

11

~~~~~~

PLANNING TO RETURN TO WORK

Many mothers return to the work force shortly after the birth of a baby. Whether you plan to return to work out of economic necessity, an emotional need to be employed, or to save your place on the corporate ladder, the birth of multiples adds another dimension to the decision and any child care arrangements. Child care arrangements should be made during pregnancy. Most mothers are too busy and too tired after their multiples' births.

A multiple pregnancy and childbirth is more stressful for a woman's body than the pregnancy and birth of a single baby. The more babies you are expecting, the more stressful it becomes. You will need time to recuperate and heal. You will probably get less sleep than the mother of a single baby. Your time with each baby is already divided when relating to more than one. Returning to work divides your time and energy even more. Spending a lot of time with your babies during the early months is essential if you are to get to know the individual babies, so build babies' time into your employment plans. (See Keys 20 and 21 for more information.)

Review Your Options

As you make employment plans, consider options that minimize child-care costs and expenses yet provide babies with optimal care. It may be helpful to consider the following questions.

- After deducting child care costs and other job-related expenses, how much disposable income will you really have? The birth of multiples may mean that it costs almost as much for both parents to work as it does for one to stay home, at least until they are toddlers. Child care for infant multiples is generally very expensive. When you add up the cost of child care, a working wardrobe, transportation to and from work and meals out, staying home may cost less than imagined.

- You may want to consider postponing the return to work. Can you extend the maternity leave? Would taking an unpaid leave of absence be an option? The Family and Medical Leave Act of 1993 requires covered employers to grant eligible employees up to 12 weeks of unpaid leave during any 12-month period for the birth or adoption of a child. If both parents work for a covered employer, each may take 12 weeks consecutively, which will give babies six months total care with a full-time parent.

- Can work schedules be arranged so that one or the other parent is home with the babies most of the day? Can either parent switch to an afternoon shift? Would an employer agree to a flex-time arrangement? If you think a specific arrangement will work better for your family, it cannot hurt to ask.

- Would an employer be open to the concept of job sharing if you and another coworker each worked part time at the same job? Although it may not be the company policy now, some companies are willing to be flexible because job sharing between two trained employees is more cost-effective than training someone new.

- Would working part-time rather than full-time for awhile benefit you and your babies? This arrangement allows for extra time with the babies, gives your body more time to recover, and allows you to remain visible in the work force. Perhaps you might work part-time hours while your spouse takes over at home.

- Do you have a skill that would enable you to earn money working from home? You will need a mother's helper during work time, but you are there for emergencies and to offer a helping hand when needed, while still gainfully employed.

Considerations

Although grandparents may love your children almost as much as you do, and some may be the first choice as a childcare

43

provider, others may not be up to the task of watching so many or they may not be able to continue long term. With today's transient society, many grandparents simply are not available. Consider the following when you think about day care.

- Ultimately, you are responsible for your children even when someone else watches them part of the day. Be certain any child-care provider clearly understands your expectations with regard to raising multiples and developing individuality.
- Consider live-in child-care help if employed full time. This option is no longer reserved for the wealthy, especially when you calculate the cost of day care for more than one child. Many families of multiples have also had successful experiences with an au pair.
- You will want to hire someone who adores babies and will interact with each infant. If this person comes to your home, do not expect her to perform light housekeeping as well. She will not have the time when caring for multiples.
- If babies are going to a day-care provider, consider finding one close to the workplace instead of close to home. You gain time to interact with the babies during travel, and occasionally you may be able to visit them during the workday for a feeding. This is especially helpful for the breastfeeding mother. (See Keys 15, 16, and 18.)
- Are you able to make special arrangements for day care if the babies are sick? Studies show that children in day care are ill more often than children who remain in their own homes. Many parents use their own sick days when children are ill, but between/among them, multiples may be sick so often that parents run out of sick days.
- Interview several care givers. Although some providers charge less for each subsequent baby in a family, child care is not the place to scrimp. You are placing precious possessions in the sitter's care.
- For higher-order multiples, one childcare provider may not be enough. Parents may have to hire two (or more) at least during their multiples' infancy.

12

~~~~~~

D(ELIVERY) DAY

The big day is finally here. Today is your babies' birthday whether Mother Nature alone decides the date or she is given a nudge by you and your obstetrical care provider(s). If you are like most parents of multiples, you have been looking forward to this day with both excitement and some trepidation.

Hospital Admission

Hospital birth, supervised by an accredited obstetrician, is recommended for all multiple births. Also, many obstetric care providers advise giving vaginal birth to twins (or triplets) in a delivery room equipped for an emergency cesarean rather than in a "homelike" birthing room, because there is no way to anticipate exactly how a second multiple will engage, or become positioned, in the birth canal until after the first baby is delivered.

Obstetric care providers send information about each expectant mother and her pregnancy history to the hospital labor and delivery unit, so the staff is prepared for multiples. This information may not be available if labor is preterm. Be sure to take several copies of any birth plan developed; they usually are not included with material sent to the hospital in advance. Review details of any plan with your labor nurse. (See Key 2.)

Labor and delivery staff prepare for all birth possibilities.

- Ultrasound may be used to check each baby's current position.
- Blood work is drawn and a urine specimen obtained during admission for lab analysis.
- An intravenous (IV) line usually is placed in one arm during active labor, although this is not always attached to a bag of IV fluid. When an unmedicated birth is planned, a mother may ask for an IV heparin lock instead, which interferes less with movement but ensures that a vein is accessible for any emergency.

- When a surgical (cesarean) delivery is planned, a urinary catheter will be inserted during admission. This procedure may be done at the last moment for an emergency surgical delivery.
- Vaginal examination is performed during admission and periodically thereafter to check the degree of the opening (dilatation) in the *cervix*. The cervix must dilate completely to 10 centimeters for a baby to pass out of the uterus vaginally. After the cervix has dilated 10 cm, it still is necessary to move a baby farther down the birth canal toward the vaginal opening by pushing during contractions.
- Electronic fetal monitoring (EFM) of each baby is recommended at the time of admission and during active labor. This monitoring may be done for 20 or 30 minutes of each hour if a mother wishes to walk and the babies are responding well to labor. Continuous monitoring is recommended during the later phases of first stage labor or when any baby's response to labor is in question.

    Monitoring can be done externally via belts (one belt per multiple) with sensors that pick up each baby's heart tones and a belt with a device sensitive to uterine contractions. The belts are connected to fetal monitoring machines that record babies' heart rates and the uterine contractions on a graph.

    Internal monitoring of the multiple in the birth canal may be done to get a more accurate recording of that baby's heart rate. Internal monitoring is possible only after this multiple's membranes, or bag of waters, has broken (ruptured). Sometimes a labor and delivery staff member ruptures this amniotic sac to attach an internal monitoring device to the baby in the birth canal.

Labor

Labor occurs in several stages:

- The *first stage* begins with contractions that affect the cervix. The cervix thins (effaces) and dilates, so that each baby's body can pass through it, one after the other, into the birth canal for delivery. Generally, the cervix remains open once it has completely dilated, so most mothers giving birth to multiples do not have to cope with the contractions of first-stage labor more than once.

- During the *second stage*, the laboring woman pushes the baby in the birth canal down and out of the vaginal opening for the actual birth. This process must be repeated for each multiple. After the birth of the first multiple, the next "in line" must get positioned in the birth canal and be pushed through and out. With rare exceptions, all babies are born before any placenta is expelled.
- The *third stage* begins with the birth of the last baby and continues until the one large or all separate placentas are expelled from the uterus, usually within 10 or 15 minutes of the last birth.
- A *fourth stage* begins when all placentas are expelled and lasts until a woman's physical system is stable and obviously adapting to the changes occurring with birth. For most women this lasts one to four hours.

Myth has it that labor often lasts longer for women carrying multiples. This is not so. In fact, one study found that the length of labor for women having twins was slightly less than the labors of women giving birth to a single baby. However, for some women, the overdistention of the uterus that occurs with multiples seems to result in less efficient contractions, which may prolong labor.

It is not uncommon to receive medication in the IV to induce or augment (accelerate) labor. This medication can increase the intensity of uterine contractions, which may affect the degree of pain felt and a woman's ability to cope. The increase in contraction intensity also may affect one or more of the babies because contractions influence blood flow through the placenta(s). There can be good reasons for inducing or augmenting labor with multiples, but a woman should discuss the reason, and the possible risks versus benefits, that labor *induction* or *augmentation* is recommended.

Vaginal Birth

The vaginal birth of Baby A is essentially the same as the birth of a single infant. The uterus often takes several minutes to rest before readjusting "around" Baby B and before second-stage contractions begin again. The position of any subsequent multiple cannot be determined absolutely until the birth of the multiple "in front" of it. The second multiple cannot engage, become positioned, in the birth canal before the birth of the first baby. (Any triplet Baby C could not engage in the pelvis until after Baby B is born.)

Multiples usually are born several minutes to several hours apart. The average time between births is about 10 to 40 minutes. (In very rare instances, the multiples in a set have been born days to months apart.) The time between the births is not an issue when it is possible to monitor any baby still in the uterus. Trying to "hurry up" the birth of a subsequent multiple should be avoided unless the baby is showing signs of distress.

When a surgical delivery is performed for a set of multiples, the birth of the second (third, fourth, and so on) multiple quickly follows the birth of the one before it.

Vaginal Versus Surgical (Cesarean) Birth

The surgical birth rate for multiples is high. About 50 percent of both twins and another 10 percent of second twins only are surgically delivered. Some obstetricians routinely perform surgical deliveries for all twin pregnancies. Some do this in case the second twin is breech. However, research does not support routine surgical delivery as safer for twins when the first twin is vertex, or head first, in the birth canal, and the first twin is vertex in more than 80 percent of twin pregnancies. The delivery route for a twin birth should be determined by the circumstances of an individual pregnancy and labor. One delivery method does not fit all.

The surgical delivery rate may be close to 100 percent for higher-order multiple sets that are beyond 24 weeks gestation at the time of delivery. Although there is a trend in some non-U.S. countries toward "trial of labor" for triplet pregnancies if Baby A is vertex, the available research indicates better infant outcomes after surgical birth for triplets and other higher-order multiples.

Labor Medication and Anesthesia Options

Unmedicated labor and birth, sometimes called natural childbirth, is often possible for the vaginal birth of one or both twins. It is occasionally considered when triplets are born vaginally. Obstetric care providers may encourage an unmedicated birth with twins because the laboring mother is usually able to push more effectively during second-stage labor, which decreases the likelihood that (outlet) forceps or vacuum extraction will be needed.

This can be especially beneficial for delivery of the second twin. Also, the lack of exposure to medication during labor and birth is considered beneficial for the babies. *Episiotomy*, an incision to enlarge the vaginal opening, is less likely to be performed for unmedicated vertex births.

A woman planning an unmedicated twin birth should be aware that it occasionally becomes necessary to use general anesthesia to put a mother to sleep if there is a difficulty or an emergency when delivering a second twin. In such situations, the obstetrician may have to reach up in the vagina and uterus to help the second twin, so a local anesthetic wouldn't be of use. There would not be time to administer an epidural or spinal anesthetic.

A *spinal* or *saddle block* is an anesthetic given immediately before the birth of the first baby or just before beginning a surgical birth procedure. It allows a woman to remain conscious and alert for birth. This anesthesia provides good pain relief for delivery, but it offers no relief for most of the labor. Women usually are told to lie flat for several hours to prevent spinal headache.

When a woman requests a pain reliever for contractions, a *narcotic medication* usually is given. Different narcotics are used more often in different areas of the country. Different dosages may be used for different women. These medications generally are given intramuscularly (IM) or through the IV tubing. A narcotic also may be given as part of epidural medication.

Epidural anesthesia is often considered the method of choice for multiple births: (1) it generally offers good pain relief during labor and delivery; (2) it can be used if a surgical delivery becomes necessary; and (3) most mothers can sit to hold and breastfeed the babies immediately after the birth. Epidurals differ. Sometimes only a "numbing" type medication is used; sometimes a narcotic medication is added to that.

Less ability to "feel" the urge to push and the effort of pushing during second-stage labor may be a possible disadvantage of epidural anesthesia. When this occurs, it may result in the use of forceps or vacuum extraction for the birth of one or both twins. A mother's blood pressure is watched closely for a large drop during epidural anesthesia, which can also affect placental function.

All medications used during labor for pain relief or as anesthetic agents affect the babies while they remain in the uterus. A local block of numbing medication used to perform an episiotomy is the only exception. The degree of medication effect may vary between, or among, the babies. Also, some medications have more obvious effects than others. As with any medication babies are exposed to, risks versus benefits must be considered.

Labor Support

Usually, a woman's partner—her husband or another support person—may remain with her throughout labor and vaginal or surgical delivery. In many hospitals, a woman may have additional people during her labor and vaginal birth. If a vaginal birth of one or more is likely, consider hiring a *doula* to attend the birth(s). A doula is trained to work with the woman and her partner during labor and birth. She will know any birth plan thoroughly, so she also is able to work with the staff to see that the couple's plan is carried out. This allows the laboring woman to concentrate on the work of labor. Research has shown that women who have a doula tend to have shorter labors with less medication and fewer complications.

To locate a trained support person or doula service, check the phone book or ask a childbirth education instructor for information. Some midwives act as doulas when one of their clients is carrying multiples and must be referred to an obstetrician for supervision of pregnancy, labor, and birth. (Also, see Appendix B: Resources—Birth and Postpartum Support: Doulas.)

Expecting the Unexpected

The most predictable thing about multiple births is their unpredictability. All medical judgments concerning labor and birth should be discussed with the laboring woman and her husband. A woman is more likely to relax and trust the obstetrician's decisions about her individual labor when she and the obstetrician have been working together throughout the pregnancy. (See Key 2.)

13

‸‸

IMMEDIATE POSTPARTUM PERIOD

The days immediately after birth are a period of great change. A woman's body shifts gears as it adapts to babies' swift exit and prepares to make milk during lactation. Mentally, a woman begins to integrate the pregnancy, labor, and birth experiences with the reality of the babies' arrival.

Physical Changes

Vaginal bleeding is the most obvious sign that the body has switched gears after birth, and it occurs whether a woman has had a vaginal or surgical (cesarean) birth. *Excessive bleeding* or actual *postpartum hemorrhage* is more common after a multiple birth. The uterus needs to contract more effectively, since more of the uterus was covered by placental tissue; however, it may not contract well after stretching to accommodate multiple babies.

- Notify a nurse if you fill more than one sanitary pad in an hour or if you pass a blood clot larger than a golf ball.
- Check your uterus several times the first few days to be sure it is contracting well. It will feel like a hard grapefruit in the middle of your abdomen. Each day it will feel smaller and lower in your abdomen. If it does not feel hard or bleeding increases, rub over the uterus, or in the middle of your abdomen, until you feel it harden.
- Afterbirth cramps (contractions) may be stronger for a day or two after giving birth to multiples. Also, you may feel these menstrual-like cramps more strongly during the first day or two of breastfeeding, which is a positive sign that milk "let-down" is

occurring. Medication that causes cramping may be given if health care providers think bleeding is excessive.

- Bleeding often increases days or weeks after giving birth when a new mother tries to do too much too soon. This may be her body's way of saying, "Sit down and prop your feet up. Don't be Superwoman." Wearing a robe rather than "regular" clothing for the first weeks after childbirth is a good way to remind yourself and others that you are still recuperating from a multiple pregnancy and birth. Report continued bleeding to the obstetric provider.

If experiencing swelling or pain in the perineum (pubic area) during the first 24 hours postpartum, ask to have an *ice* bag placed between your legs. After 24 hours, *warm water* may feel more comfortable and encourage healing. Women can apply warm water to the perineum by using a squirt bottle or a sitz bath, and by letting water spray on the area during a shower. Many women report that warm water feels especially good if they experienced swelling or soreness in the perineal area during the last weeks of pregnancy.

Consider the following after a *surgical delivery.*

- Alternatives in immediate *postoperative pain relief* (analgesia) allow women to get up and begin to care for their babies the first day. Among the common alternatives is a one-time injection of a narcotic into the epidural space. Most women get good pain relief that lasts about 24 hours. Although excessive itching for several hours is a fairly common side effect, another medication can be given to minimize this.

Patient-controlled analgesia (PCA) pumps allow small amounts of narcotic medication to be released slowly through an intravenous (IV) line. Women who have used a PCA pump report varying levels of pain relief; some get good relief and others report it had little effect. Most felt drowsy while they used it. Many new mothers were too groggy to care for their babies until it was discontinued.

In some areas women are given intramuscular (IM) injections of certain nonsteroidal anti-inflammatory (NSAID) analgesics. These injections provide good pain relief, yet they have no effect on consciousness, so a mother can begin to care for her babies.

- An *oral pain medication* (analgesic) usually provides good pain relief for most women within 24 to 36 hours of a surgical birth. Notify the nurse or your doctor if you are not getting the pain relief you need with the oral analgesic prescribed.
- New mothers suggest cushioning the incision site with pillows to protect it from accidental bumps when holding and feeding babies and when changing position in bed.

New mothers pass large amounts of urine and often perspire excessively in the first days after birth, and the new mother of multiples may pass even more. This is the body's way of *eliminating the extra blood volume* acquired during multiple pregnancy. This contributes to the significant loss in the first week of pounds (kg) gained during pregnancy.

Initiating frequent *breastfeeding*, or breast *pumping*, as soon after birth as possible is the best way to increase breast-milk production, improve uterine contracting, and avoid severe engorgement or sore nipples. When you and your twins or triplets are healthy and able to breastfeed frequently after birth:

- Insist that all babies be brought to you for all breastfeedings, including at night.
- Ask family members to take turns staying with you so the babies can room in with you. This is very helpful after a surgical birth.
- If one twin or triplet cannot yet go to breast, breastfeed one baby who can and try to pump the other breast simultaneously. Many mothers find they express more milk this way.

Establish a *breast-pumping routine* if initial breastfeeding is delayed. If pumping is difficult because you are experiencing complications or discomfort after a surgical delivery, ask nurses or a family member to apply the pump every few hours.

Although some women experience *nipple tenderness* with breastfeeding in the first week after birth, extreme nipple soreness or nipple cracking usually is related to improper positioning of one or more multiples at the breast or a feeding difficulty that interferes with effective breastfeeding for one or more.

If *severe breast engorgement* occurs, *move milk* out of the breasts through frequent breastfeeding or pumping. Some women say milk flows more easily if they apply warm compresses for a minute or two before breastfeeding. Because swelling of breast tissue is part of severe engorgement, apply *cold compresses* or ice bags around each breast between feedings or after pumping. (Place a towel over the breasts and the compresses or ice bags over the towel.) Relieving the swelling can get the milk moving again.

Contact a lactation consultant (IBCLC) or a breastfeeding support group leader experienced with multiple births immediately if you need help initiating breastfeeding or breast pumping or if you experience any breastfeeding difficulty. (For information about contacting breastfeeding support professionals in a specific location, see Appendix B: Resources—Breastfeeding/Lactation.)

It can be exciting to see and feel what appears to be a now-flat abdomen while still lying down after giving birth, but excitement may turn to surprise or dismay the first time you stand up. Don't panic if you look several months pregnant after giving birth!

- The body produced more of the hormone that helps loosen skin to stretch and accommodate the growth of multiple babies during pregnancy, and it may take time for the body to eliminate all traces of those "skin-loosening" hormones. Abdominal skin may feel loose for several months but it will improve.
- If abdominal skin looks puckered, you may have acquired what some call "twin skin" or "seersucker skin"! Some of the elasticity may have been lost when stretching for a multiple pregnancy. Twin skin is more common after delivering full-term, or close to full-term, babies having average birth weights.
- The vertical muscle (rectus abdominus) that runs down the center of the abdomen actually is two muscles that often separate as the pregnant uterus grows. This muscle separation is called a *diastasis recti*, and one can feel the space between the abdominal muscles when lifting the head off the bed. It often resolves within several months of birth. A multiple pregnancy can exaggerate diastasis recti, especially when the babies' combined birth weight is over 10 pounds (4.5 kg), and the separation may remain even with exercise to tone abdominal muscles. Because effects to

long-term posture and herniation are possible, discuss diastasis recti with your health-care provider if it persists beyond babies' first birthday.

Emotional Changes

An expectant mother may have seen her multiples many times on ultrasound. She may have been a master at recognizing their separate movements. She watched her abdomen overexpand as the babies grew inside her. Yet most women still find it difficult to believe that two, three, four, or more babies could actually be inside them until they can see all the babies together. It is difficult to absorb that multiple babies are really here until you begin to touch and hold them.

- It is important to see and care for all babies together from birth when possible so the idea of multiple newborns becomes physically real. Total or partial rooming-in makes this easier when twins, and some triplets, are full/close to full term and all are in good physical condition. In many hospitals, a family member or friend can stay with you at all times to help with babies.
- If one or more multiples must be transferred to the NICU, ask the nurse to place them side-by-side so you can see them together before the transfer, unless it is an emergency. Your husband or the nurse can photograph them together if there is time. The birth of the anticipated number of multiples may seem less a reality if separated from any of them. (See Keys 14 and 21.)
- It is normal to want to know if same-sex multiples are identical or fraternal. It is as much a part of who those babies are as eye color, body build, or temperament. However, it is often impossible to determine twin type at birth. (See Key 19.)
- Most new mothers want to rehash the details of the multiple pregnancy, labor, and birth with anyone willing to listen. This is a necessary and normal aspect of organizing and integrating these special events in a woman's memory.

Pregnancy lasts several months, and a woman's postpartum body needs at least several months to return to normal. Although physical and emotional change begins immediately after childbirth, the process of change continues throughout the postpartum year.

14

BABIES IN THE NICU

Many twins arrive before 36 weeks and weigh less than 5 pounds, 8 ounces. Higher-order multiples usually arrive earlier. Yet many expectant parents are surprised when this happens. If your babies are smaller than anticipated, one or more may need to be in a newborn or neonatal intensive care unit (NICU, often pronounced "nick-you"). (See Key 3.)

Even if the babies' conditions are stable, having babies in a NICU is an unfamiliar and often frightening situation for most parents. If your babies have medical problems, you may experience incredible emotional highs and lows when the babies have dramatic positive and negative changes in their conditions. You may find yourself rejoicing with good news about one baby while anguishing over bad news about another. To insulate yourself from the pain of possibly losing one, you may remain detached. Interaction and bonding can be more difficult.

What to Expect
- Until each baby is in stable condition and gaining weight steadily, a baby generally remains in the hospital. Your babies may not be able to come home together.
- You may find it especially difficult to form an attachment to one or more babies. Many mothers report feeling closer to a healthier multiple or one that is ready for eye contact or cuddling sooner. (See Key 21.)
- Sometimes a father feels closer to premature babies because he often must take control and begin visiting the NICU while mother recuperates from childbirth. Some mothers report feelings of inadequacy if babies' prematurity is coupled with what she considers to be a poor birth experience.

Suggestions

- Learn all you can about premature/preterm babies and their care. Ask questions of the staff. If you tend to think of questions at home and forget them when you get to the NICU, keep a special notebook to write questions as they come to you and then also use it to write the answers. Read books or pamphlets that explain about NICU care and equipment. (See Appendix A: Suggested Reading. The parents of multiples' organizations listed in Appendix B may also have pamphlets available.)

- Visit often. You and your babies need this contact. If the sights and sounds of the NICU seem frightening, remember that your babies need you. Before you know it, it will be familiar.

- Ask the nursery staff to place the babies' isolettes or cribs side-by-side, which makes it easier to visit all of them at once. It also reinforces the reality of giving birth to more than one baby, and many parents believe it helped them bond with all their babies.

- Ask the staff to start *co-bedding* once the physical conditions of twins, or at least two babies of a higher-order set, are stable. During co-bedding, two or more multiples are placed together in a single crib. Co-bedding seems to help multiples regulate and, in some cases, stabilize their breathing and body temperatures. It also may help them develop similar sleep-wake patterns.

- Take pictures of the babies together and separately. If you cannot yet visit your babies, or cannot visit them as often as you would like because of your own need to recuperate, ask others to take photos. Most NICUs keep an instant camera on the unit so pictures can be sent to a mother who cannot yet visit. Usually a nurse will offer to take pictures, but ask if no one offers.

- Ask the staff to help you begin *Kangaroo care* with each baby as soon as possible, which may be earlier than you think. Sometimes infants classified as very low birth weight (VLBW) or ones that are still on ventilators qualify for Kangaroo care if they are otherwise stable. During Kangaroo care, one or more babies is placed chest-to-chest, skin-to-skin with either parent. Kangaroo care has many benefits for babies, as it helps them regulate body temperature, and heart and respiratory functions. It also appears to promote babies' brain development. Parents say it helps them feel closer to each baby, and they feel better knowing they are doing something important for each baby.

- When you cannot visit, call frequently for updates. Ask about each baby separately. You never have to worry that it may be too late or too early to call. Someone is there caring for your babies around the clock, and NICU staff members are glad when parents care enough to be concerned at any hour.

- Call each baby by his or her given name. This makes the idea of multiple babies seem more real. It also helps you and the staff think of each baby as an individual. Do not refer to any baby by a label, such as "the boy," "the smaller baby," or "the sicker baby." This may be a way of insulating and distancing yourself from the pain of having a sick baby.

- Concentrate on more than the multiples' individual medical reports. Notice how each responds to being fed, changed, turned, or examined. What actions calm and which upset each?

- If a staff member refers to them as Baby A or Baby B (or Baby C or Baby D) or the "twins" (the "triplets," the "quads"), take the initiative and ask specific questions about each baby by name. Let them know you consider each to be an individual.

- Leave something that has your scent, such as a handkerchief or breast pad, in each isolette or crib.

- Multiples often are discharged at different times because babies' conditions are not exactly the same. Many mothers report feeling closer to whichever baby came home first. This may be because the mother can concentrate on that baby without also having to care for another. If you are aware of this natural reaction, you can take steps to remedy it. (See Key 22.)

- Buy special outfits designed for preterm babies. It is amazing how much better your babies look, and how much better you may feel, when they are dressed in something that fits! (See Appendix B: Resources—General Shopping.)

Feeding Your Premature Babies

Many parents say they do not feel the babies are actually theirs until they begin to feed them, so ask to do this as soon as possible and keep asking. Do not let tubes and equipment get in the way of enjoying this nurturing experience. A nurse will show you how to hold your babies. Do not postpone contact with your babies until you are all home. You will gain confidence in handling multiples if you begin early.

Your breast milk is especially beneficial when multiples are preterm or ill at birth, so if you planned to breastfeed, do not give up the idea now. Preterm milk is different than milk produced for full-term babies, and it is perfect for your premature infants. Preterm or sick babies who receive their mothers' milk have fewer and milder infections, and many experts now encourage all mothers to provide their milk for their preterm babies.

Even if you didn't plan to breastfeed, consider giving your multiples the advantages of your milk by pumping your breasts for their first several weeks or months. You may need extra support when you express your milk for your babies. NICU staff members should know how to help you contact a certified lactation consultant (IBCLC) or local La Leche League leader who can coach you in how to use a breast pump, store and transport your milk, and later offer help when each baby is ready to breastfeed. They also can help you work with medical personnel, and they will continue to offer advice and support when the babies come home. (See Appendix B: Resources—Breastfeeding/Lactation.)

Whether they are fed by bottle or breast, preterm babies need to be fed more frequently than full-term babies. They usually take smaller amounts at each feeding, although it often takes these little babies longer to feed. You may feel more confident about breastfeeding if you rent a digital scale that allows you to see how much each baby took with a breastfeeding by weighing each before and after some of their breastfeedings.

Home

When you bring your babies home, you may find you experience more anxiety than the mother of full-term babies or the mother of a single baby born prematurely. These suggestions should help ease the transition:

- If possible, have a home health nurse visit you and the babies. She can reassure you if all is well, and she will know what may be helpful if you or any baby continues to have a health problem. Your babies' pediatric care provider can help secure some type of ongoing respite care if any baby comes home with a health issue still requiring round-the-clock care.

- Get help with household tasks so you can devote all your attention to your babies. Both you and they need time together.
- Keep visitors to a minimum until you and the babies are stronger and you have established some kind of routine. A good reason for limiting visitors with preterm or sick newborns is that they are more susceptible to infection. This may be especially important during the months of October to May when Respiratory Syncytial Virus (RSV) occurs more often. RSV is a respiratory illness that produces symptoms similar to a cold for those over a year old. However, infants, especially those who were born preterm, often are affected by a more severe form of this virus. Babies are less likely to develop RSV if breastfed or breast-milk fed. If they do contract it, the symptoms tend to be less severe.
- During the day, keep babies together where you can see them even while they sleep. This reinforces that you are now the parents of multiples and allows you to respond to each as quickly as possible. If one awakens, even for a few moments, pick her up and cuddle only her.
- Your babies need contact with you even if they do not seem to crave it, and you need contact with them even if it does not feel natural at first.

Do not blame yourself for your babies' preterm birth. Few mothers did anything to cause this, and rarely is there anything they might have done that would have prevented it. Guilt is unproductive. The time and attention you might waste on feeling guilty is better spent getting to know your babies. After a few months, any worry you might have felt will begin to fade and you can relax and experience the trials and joys that all parents of multiples experience. It may help to remember that patience, determination, and an acceptance that your feelings are normal reactions to an unusual situation can overcome even the poorest beginning.

15

BREASTFEED OR BOTTLE-FEED?

C hoosing a feeding method is one of the biggest decisions expectant parents make, and probably one of the most controversial. No other topic may stimulate as much discussion as whether to feed by breast or bottle. Everyone has an opinion, often based as much on emotion as fact. But this is *your* decision.

There is no question that with rare exceptions "breast milk is best milk." Study after study shows that Mother Nature designed human milk for human babies. Yet every mother, baby, and family is different. Only you can judge what feeding method, or combination of methods, may work best in your situation.

No matter which feeding method you choose, multiple babies will take more time and effort. Also, feeding means much more than food for both you and your babies. Feedings not only meet your babies' physiological need for food, they are mealtimes, and mealtime is traditionally a time for socializing. They provide you with an opportunity to respond to each baby's cues, to hold each one close, and to interact and maintain eye contact. These actions let a baby know he is loved, which enables each baby to feel safe, secure, and valued. Feeding interactions help you get to know the babies as individuals.

Feedings also show your babies that they have some control over their environment and trust it to meet their needs. (You are part of the environment.) Each learns this as he feels hunger and works up tension, which he demonstrates in the form of feeding cues, such as licking, rooting, bringing hands to face, and finally crying. When his cues are answered quickly, he discovers he can make things happen in his environment. He comes to trust you, the consistent caregiver, since you are the one who usually answers his cues by picking him up and feeding him to relieve hunger pangs.

If any baby's cues (communications) are often ignored, the bottle (or breast) is frequently propped, or any baby is frequently exposed to different caregivers, he learns to think of himself as an inadequate signal sender. He learns he cannot trust himself or his environment when his cues do not produce a predictable response.

Nature designed infant feedings as an activity to be repeated many times a day, giving you many opportunities to fulfill your babies' basic physiological and emotional needs. Both needs are important. Neither diminishes or disappears because a baby arrives as part of a set or a feeding method allows for propping the food supply or passing babies around to numerous caregivers.

Your responsibility to meet each baby's emotional as well as physical needs does not change when you give birth to more than one baby. This is not to imply that no one else should ever help you feed your babies or that bottles should never be propped; in fact, doing either occasionally might better meet your babies' immediate needs. However, you must become particularly conscientious and not lose sight of your babies emotional and physical needs in the reasonable quest for organization and efficiency.

Points to Consider

Among the advantages of breastfeeding are:

- Breastfeeding ensures that you and your babies are in close contact many times a day, providing opportunities for you to get to know each baby as an individual.
- Breast milk is nutritionally superior. It is digested more easily and more completely than any artificial formula, which is less stressful for immature babies' systems.
- Breast milk contains several anti-infective properties and anti-allergic factors that cannot be duplicated in artificial formulas. This is helpful in avoiding illness with multiples, because they often share contagious diseases.

- Breastfeeding is more economical. The extra calories you need cost much less than formula, and usually no expensive equipment is required. Even if you buy or rent a hospital-grade electric breast pump to use initially or for many months, this still costs hundreds of dollars less than artificial formulas.
- Breastfeeding requires no preparation, refrigeration, or clean up. It is always available and it is always at the right temperature.
- Many mothers say the frequent feedings give them an excuse to sit and rest during the day, which is an important part of recuperating from a multiple pregnancy and birth.
- The uterus contracts during breastfeeding or pumping, helping to limit bleeding during the early postpartum period. Breastfeeding usually delays the return of the menstrual cycle, which also helps a new mother recover by limiting blood loss.

The advantages of bottle-feeding with pumped breast milk or formula include:

- Mother can have help with feedings. Each parent can concentrate totally on one baby, unless babies in higher-order sets want to eat at once. This lets both parents discover their infants as individuals.
- Fathers have more opportunity to become involved. Dad can take over feeding during the night, giving Mom time to recoup her strength after childbirth or after a few nights "on call" herself. You may have more energy after a good night's rest. (See Key 34.)
- You may need to measure how much nourishment your babies are getting, especially if they were preterm.
- If you leave your multiples with a sitter, you know their need for food can be easily met and they are more likely to be content.

Infant feedings play a critical role in laying the foundation for behavioral patterns that continue long after you and your multiples move on to other stages of development. Don't let feedings become task-oriented and inflexibly organized. Ensure that babies' emotional and physical needs are met during feedings.

16

~~~~~~

BREASTFEEDING

Nature designed the human female so that most women could breastfeed several babies. Many women have breast-fed twins and quite a few have breastfed triplets or quadruplets. Ignore those who say, "You can't possibly make enough milk for two (three, four) babies," or "It will be too hard on you and your family to *try* to nurse twins (triplets, quadruplets)."

You *can* breastfeed no matter what the circumstances. If a stress-free postpartum period was a requirement for breastfeeding success, few mothers of multiples could meet it!

Breastfeeding multiples requires an understanding of breast milk production, a commitment to continue through the early adjustment period, and a support network to cheer you on if you become discouraged or frustrated. When issues related to having multiple infants are separated from breastfeeding issues, most mothers discover that breastfeeding can be one of the least complicated aspects of caring for multiple infants.

Human milk production operates on the principle that infant *demand determines supply*. The more each baby breastfeeds, the more milk the breasts produce. The less each baby breastfeeds and any is supplemented, the less milk produced in the breasts.

Getting Started

Feed each baby as soon after birth as possible and frequently thereafter for full-term, or close to term, twins or triplets. Early, frequent feedings by two or more babies let the breasts know to produce the amount of milk needed for multiples. (Information for getting started with preterm twins is included later in this Key.)

Let each baby's feeding cues, not the clock, determine when to feed any multiple. For instance, offer the breast when any appears to "root" or seek the breast, makes licking or sucking movements, or brings hands to face or mouth. Crying is a late feeding cue. Cue, or "demand," feeding is a baby's way of telling its mother's body how much milk to make.

Healthy, alert babies breastfeed about 8 to 12 times in 24 hours. If you wonder whether each multiple is getting enough to eat, keep an eye on wet and dirty diapers. By the end of their first week, each baby should produce *at least* six wet and three dirty diapers in each 24-hour period. Many parents monitor feedings and diaper counts by using a simple checklist chart for each baby. Copying charts on different colored papers and assigning a certain color for each baby makes it easier to keep track.

Overcoming Complications

When a mother of any multiple experiences a complication and breastfeeding initiation is delayed more than 12 to 24 hours, begin expressing colostrum by using a hospital-grade electric breast pump with a pump "kit" that can be adapted for single or double pumping. It may be necessary to have a nurse or IBCLC show a relative or good friend how to pump a mother if treatment for a complication initially interferes with her ability to do it herself. To get milk production off to the best start when using a pump, it helps to be aware of several concepts.

- Not all breast pumps are equal. Hospital-grade pumps, which can be rented, were designed to establish and maintain full milk production. Most mini-electric, battery, or manual breast pumps cannot do the job.
- Ideally, a mother pumps her milk as often or for as long as a healthy newborn, which is about 8 to 12 times or 100 to 140 minutes in 24 hours with no more than one four- to five-hour period without pumping. When a mother's condition interferes with "ideal" milk expression for the first few days, she should increase the number of pumping sessions as soon as possible.
- Mothers should consider 8 pumping sessions in 24 hours as the *minimum* number needed to establish and maintain milk pro-

duction for the equivalent of one baby. Pumping less is likely to result in low milk production. Most mothers can increase milk production by increasing the number of pumping sessions.

- Because a higher level of milk production will be needed to feed multiple newborns, a new mother of multiples should aim for 10 to 12 pumping sessions in 24 hours. A mother can gradually add pumping sessions as she recuperates or babies require more milk.

- The "average" pumping session lasts about 10 to 20 minutes. Many mothers recommend applying warm compresses followed by breast massage before beginning to pump both breasts at once. (Massage even when there isn't time for warm compresses.) Some mothers pump continuously for 10 to 20 minutes; others find they get more milk if they take a break when the initial milk flow slows and then resume pumping.

- Some mothers prefer to pump one side at a time, especially when first learning. Pump both breasts twice by alternating the right and left breasts (for about 3 to 7 minutes, depending on milk flow) and then pumping each again. This technique often takes a few extra minutes, but it may be easier to manage initially and the mother can massage one breast as she pumps. Once milk "comes in," many mothers switch to pumping both breasts at once.

- A few mothers, especially those with higher-order multiples, report experiencing a *delay* in copious milk production. Instead of the usual three to five days, their milk does not "come in" for seven to ten days. Occasionally, it doesn't occur for weeks. No certain factor, complication, or treatment of multiple pregnancy or birth has been identified as a cause. Although it doesn't appear to be the only factor, often these mothers were not encouraged to pump frequently for the first several days after birth. Maintain the recommended breast-pumping routine even if milk volume remains lower, and discuss the issue with a lactation consultant (IBCLC).

- Plan to pump until all babies effectively breastfeed; the number or length of pumping sessions decreases as breastfeeding improves.

- *Maintain contact* with an IBCLC and a breastfeeding support group leader. They can provide instruction for pumping or using recommended breastfeeding devices, develop a plan for introducing breastfeeding, and offer encouragement. (See Keys 14, 18, and 30. Appendix B: Resources includes information for locating breastfeeding support and for companies with breastfeeding devices.)

Routine

Some babies regularly space breastfeedings two to three hours apart; others sleep for longer periods and then "cluster" several feedings close together. Both patterns are common, but if coping with two or three variations of normal, it can be confusing! Most babies develop fairly predictable feeding routines by six to eight weeks, although babies' patterns continue to evolve.

- Many mothers continue to breastfeed twins according to feeding cues. Some mothers of triplets also cue feed, but many recommend having a helper to take over household tasks if they are to be available for babies' frequent feedings.
- If a more "defined" schedule is required to physically manage multiples' breastfeedings, mothers often wake one baby to breastfeed immediately before, with, or after another. This routine does not work for all sets, especially when babies' feeding patterns are quite different. If it isn't practical for the early weeks or months, re-introduce it when they are a bit older.
- Cue and scheduled feedings may be combined. Some mothers "schedule" feedings during the day and feed "on cue" at night, but other mothers prefer the reverse. If scheduling at night, it is possible to miss a multiple's readiness to sleep for a longer stretch.

Never "put off" any baby to reach some ideal number of hours between feedings. To do so can interfere with milk production and babies' weight gain.

Coordinating Double, Triple, or Quadruple Breastfeedings

Almost any method of coordinating breastfeedings works when fully breastfeeding, if each baby breastfeeds at least *8 to 12* times in 24 hours. (Partial breastfeeding is discussed in Key 18.)

- The simplest routine is to offer one breast per feeding. Alternate babies and breasts every 24 hours. Assign the right breast to one and left to another for one day, and switch the following day. For quadruplets, two babies could be "assigned" the right breast and two the left breast for 24 hours.
- Mothers of triplets tend to rotate babies and breasts more often. It usually isn't necessary to keep track perfectly, as both breasts see plenty of "action" during a 24-hour period! Some mothers of even-numbered multiple sets also prefer this feeding routine.
- Some mothers of twins offer both breasts to each baby at every feeding. For example, Baby A feeds at the right breast until she "self-detaches" and then finishes on the left if still hungry. Baby B begins on the left breast and finishes on the right. Few mothers continue this beyond a few weeks, because many multiples over-feed if offered both breasts.
- For even-numbered sets, a mother may choose to assign each multiple a specific breast for all feedings, every day. However, this has created problems when one multiple could not or would not breastfeed for a few days yet another multiple wasn't willing to nurse on that one's side. Also, some women find the size of their breasts differ significantly. When this method is used, alternate feeding positions.

Simultaneous Versus Separate Feedings

Simultaneous breastfeeding, breastfeeding two babies the same age at once, is the most efficient and effective way of handling multiples' breastfeedings. However, many mothers desire the closeness of breastfeeding each baby alone. Most mothers combine methods and breastfeed two together for some feedings and feed each separately for others.

The multiples within any set usually influence whether feedings are simultaneous or separate. Their sleep-wake patterns play a role. Also, one may not cooperate with having another nearby during feedings, but another will not begin to breastfeed unless he hears the other one breastfeeding. Simultaneous feeding may be difficult during the early weeks if one or both needs mother's help

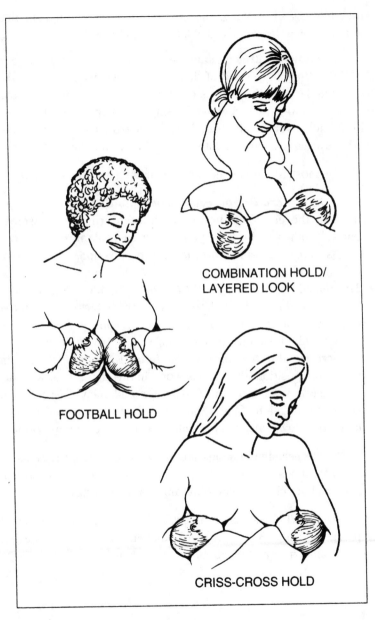

COMBINATION HOLD/
LAYERED LOOK

FOOTBALL HOLD

CRISS-CROSS HOLD

From *Breastfeeding: A Parent's Guide* (rev. ed.) by Amy K. Spangler, MN, RN, IBCLC, Atlanta, GA (1999).

with latch-on and suckling, but most multiples can be fed simultaneously when at least one easily latches and breastfeeds.

Experiment with simultaneous breastfeeding positions. (See the illustrations at the end of this Key.) Pillows placed across the lap and under a mother's arms can be used to hold babies in position. Many mothers recommend using a firmer "nursing pillow" with a wide, even "shelf" that does not narrow as it wraps under mother's arms to accommodate two babies on the pillow at once.

The most common simultaneous feeding positions include:

- *The double cradle, or criss-cross, hold:* Support a baby's head in the crook of the elbow of each arm and crisscross babies' bodies in front of you or lay each along one of your thighs. Many mothers report they use this position, or a variation of it, as babies grow older.
- *The double clutch, or football, hold:* Supporting the back of a baby's head in each hand, tuck one of the babies' bodies under each arm—along or away from the side of your body. This is the most popular position when learning to feed two at once.
- *The cradle-clutch combination hold:* Hold the first baby in the cradle position. Place the second in the clutch hold with his head gently resting on the first baby's abdomen. This position allows for a free hand and the closeness with babies that most mothers enjoy. It also lends itself more to discreet breastfeeding.

Most other simultaneous feeding positions are variations of these basic holds. These positions may be adapted for breastfeeding in a recliner chair or with older infants when lying down.

See Key 30 for ideas on breastfeeding support resources and Appendices A and B for a list of books and organizations having more detailed information about breastfeeding.

17

~~~~~~

BOTTLE-FEEDING

You can bottle-feed multiples on demand or on schedule. Some babies adapt easily to a schedule that coincides with the parents' routine; others manage better when they set their own schedules. Sometimes parents allow one baby to set the schedule for all. (If one baby needs to be fed, then all are fed even if it means waking the other(s).) What works today may need to be adjusted tomorrow, so be flexible.

Preparation

Bottles, bottle nipples, and formula, if used, should be purchased or borrowed and sterilized before the babies' birth. Post a simple chart on the refrigerator or their cribs to record the amount each baby consumes at each feeding and who is fed when. Color-coding charts (different color paper for each baby) may prevent mix-ups.

Cost Versus Convenience

Infants' nourishment is too important for experimentations. The pediatric provider can advise you on which formula(s) to use. Most standard formulas come ready to feed, concentrated, and powdered. The form chosen should balance convenience and cost.

"Ready to feed" formula is the most convenient. Simply open a can, pour the formula into a bottle, and feed the babies. It is also the most expensive.

Concentrate is easy to use and is less expensive. Liquid concentrate must be mixed with boiled or distilled water. Refrigerate the bottles of formula and any unused concentrate.

Powdered formula is the least expensive. It is not refrigerated until mixed with water. It is convenient for travel because the powder and water can be kept separate and remain unrefrigerated, until needed to feed the babies. If the powder does not dissolve completely, it may clog bottle nipples.

Bottles

You have many choices of bottles and nipples. If your babies can't use the nipples you select, try another type or brand.

Color code the bottles or caps for each baby. You then know how much each baby is eating, which bottle to grab, and which baby was fed last. With higher-order multiples, parents need more helping hands. It becomes crucial to have a *simple* organized system that all caregivers easily understand.

Feeding

Feeding one baby alone while the other(s) is pleasantly occupied is ideal since it allows for one-on-one interaction with each. If multiples readily adjust to a schedule, the other(s) may sleep or swing while one is being fed. This doesn't always happen!

If you have help with feedings, alternate the baby *you* feed even if one accepts another caregiver more readily. It is important to experience one-on-one closeness with each. This rotation should include feedings given by both parents. One father of twins always grabbed the baby who ate faster and spit up less. He began to alternate when he realized that he felt closer to the baby he always fed.

Joint Feedings

Feeding two babies together can be a time-saver. Take turns establishing eye contact with each baby. Call each by name as you become part of a love triangle. You will witness the love that exists between them as well as between you and each of them.

Joint feeding becomes easier as babies grow. You soon find positions that suit you and your babies. When you have higher-order multiples, rotate which babies feed together. These are some of the most common ways of feeding two babies together:

- You and your babies can be close and more comfortable if you feed them while you sit in bed, on a sofa, or in a large chair and the babies rest on pillows alongside your body. Some mothers use a pillow designed for breastfeeding two at once.

- Place each baby in an infant seat, sit between the babies holding a bottle in each hand, and lay one of your arms along the body of each baby while they feed. Take turns looking at and burping each baby. If infant seats seem unstable, try using a stroller or other sturdy equipment.
- Use pillows and furniture. Hold and feed one baby while the other lies beside you with her bottle propped against your leg.
- If your babies need to burp often, prop both bottles initially so you can quickly pick up and burp the baby who needs you. To prop bottles, use small blankets, towels, or clean diapers rolled up. You can also purchase bottle proppers or "no hands" feeders that attach to baby seats.

Propping bottles should be very limited. Propping is associated with ear infections. Babies held in arms are at a better angle because their heads are higher than their GI tract.

Never leave an infant unattended with a propped bottle. Infants choke easily and could aspirate fluid into their lungs. Prop bottles so babies are more comfortable, not to give you free time. Do not be lulled into a false sense of security because you have propped bottles for weeks and "nothing has ever happened." It only takes one time!

- As your babies gain strength, sit on the floor with their heads resting on one outstretched leg and their bodies between your legs. While you hold the bottles in one hand, stroke the babies' heads with the other. This position lets your babies cuddle with each other, something they may find comforting.

Not Just a Routine

Feeding should not become a chore, a task, or routine. Family mealtime is an important social gathering and sharing begins with multiples' feedings during infancy. Feeding should be a pleasant time when baby and parent have an opportunity to cement their bond and enjoy one another.

18

COMBINING BREAST
AND BOTTLE

A mother may wonder if it's possible to combine breast- and bottle-feeding. The answer is "yes." Complementary bottles or an occasional supplementary feeding can be compatible with continued breastfeeding. Frequent supplements or alternating methods for half the babies' feedings rarely works. The key to a realistic partial breastfeeding plan is understanding how the breastfeeding body works and the tradeoffs involved.

When multiple babies remove milk from the breast into their mouths during breastfeeding, they signal their mother's breasts to maintain or increase milk production. No signals can be sent if a multiple is given a bottle instead of the breast, so the mother's breasts cut back on milk production. Giving too many bottles during the early weeks and months *significantly* decreases breast milk production and is associated with early weaning.

There are tradeoffs when babies' breast-milk diet is combined with infant formula. The anti-infective and anti-allergic properties of breast milk are increasingly less effective as more formula is given. Still, partially breastfed babies have statistically fewer episodes of illness in the first year than their completely formula-fed counterparts. Some mothers continue to pump their milk so that babies may be partially breastfed, but they are completely breast-milk-fed.

Why Combine?
Multiples are more likely than single newborns to get a slow breastfeeding start because of prematurity, labor, and delivery

complications, and early mismanagement of breastfeeding. Many are still receiving their mother's expressed breast milk or infant formula when discharged from the hospital. It may be more complicated to overcome a poor breastfeeding start when caring for multiple newborns, and many mothers continue to include bottles because they don't know how to eliminate them.

Other mothers choose to "top off" (complement) or supplement breastfeeding for a variety of reasons. Some mothers have a real, and others a perceived, concern that they cannot produce enough milk for every multiple. Perhaps one or more babies need a boost after an inadequate weight gain. Because of other responsibilities, a mother may find there are not enough hours in the day for the number of breastfeedings multiples require. She might want help with some feedings, or she may use bottles if babies spend time in others' care.

Increasing Breast Milk Production

To make up for a slow start, a few days of around-the-clock breastfeeding, as each baby's sucking ability improves, is usually enough to increase milk production. If round-the-clock breastfeeding sounds overwhelming or isn't possible, slowly transition one or two at once from bottle to breast.

- Offer the breast, if possible, when any baby demonstrates feeding cues, such as licking, rooting, putting hands to face, or crying.
- Delete ½ to 1 ounce (15–30 ml) of expressed breast milk or formula per bottle per day for several days. Expect multiple(s) to cue for more breastfeeding for several days, and diaper counts may decrease briefly. Once any baby resumes an 8 to 12 feedings a day routine, delete another ½ to 1 ounce per bottle per day. Repeat until your breastfeeding goal is achieved.
- Certain breastfeeding devices can help transition babies to breast more quickly, improve milk production, or transfer milk more effectively. For instance, a *feeding tube device* at the breast, such as Medela's Supplemental Nursing System (SNS) provides supplement as one or two breastfeed. This device saves the time it takes to "top off" with a bottle after breastfeeding

and it helps increase breast milk production. A thin silicone *nipple shield* may be helpful with a multiple that has a weak or disorganized suck. Parents can rent a digital scale to weigh an infant before and after breastfeeding. *Test-weighing* is a fairly reliable way to learn how well any multiple removes milk during breastfeeding and also determine whether, and how much, additional milk may still be necessary.

• Continue to pump breasts for several minutes after breastfeeding using a hospital-grade electric *breast pump* until all babies effectively breastfeed without the help of a device. (Some mothers continue to pump so they will have their own milk for any complementary or supplementary feedings.)

• *Let helpers offer alternative feedings* to avoid feeling overwhelmed. This gives a mother more time to "practice" breastfeeding with babies and to pump frequently to maintain breast milk production.

• *Maintain contact* with an IBCLC and a breastfeeding support group leader. They can make suggestions for alternative feedings, provide instruction about breastfeeding devices, fine-tune a plan for increasing breastfeeding, and offer encouragement. (See Keys 16 and 30 and Appendix B: Resources.)

Are They Getting Enough?

Mothers often wonder if they are making enough milk for multiples, since breasts are not designed with ounce (ml) markers. If concerned whether breastfed multiples are getting enough milk, review babies' checklist charts as described in Key 16 to see if *in 24 hours* each fully (or almost fully) breastfeeding multiple *usually:*

• is satisfied with 8 to 12 breastfeedings
• soaks 6 or more diapers
• passes 3 or more loose bowel movements (stools)
• gains *at least* 1/2 ounce (15 gm).

If "yes," then a mother is producing plenty of milk!

Planning Ahead

When multiples effectively breastfeed from birth, it is better to avoid introducing bottles or infant formula until milk production is well established after several weeks of full breastfeeding. This allows babies and mother time to learn to work together to latch onto and remove milk from the breasts.

Some newborns have more difficulty latching onto the breast if they receive bottles in the early weeks. This can add time and frustration to multiples' breastfeedings. If any multiple has difficulty latching or sustaining suckling for any reason, you need extra breastfeeding support. (See Key 30 and Appendix B for more information.)

Realistic Combinations

The best partial breastfeeding strategies interfere as little as possible with breast milk production. This is a situation in which "less is more," so think complement rather than supplement. A *complement* is ½ to 2 ounces (15–60 ml) of expressed breast milk or infant formula given after or in addition to a breastfeeding. Some call complementary feeding "topping off" a feeding. A *supplement* takes the place of breastfeeding.

- Offering a complement after breastfeeding in the evening or during the night appears to have the least effect on breast-milk production. Many mothers report that milk production seems to be lower at these times or this timing allows them to get a little uninterrupted sleep, plus father is more likely to be available to help. It is not necessary to complement breastfeeding every day if one objective is to accustom babies to bottles.
- Complementing every breastfeeding usually is unnecessary, even to boost a baby's weight gain, unless the baby is still experiencing a significant sucking difficulty. Frequent complementing is time-consuming and results in decreased milk production.
- An occasional or daily supplement should have minimal effect on breast milk production if each multiple breastfeeds *at least* seven to eight times a day. However, missing or delaying a feeding when producing milk for multiples may contribute to uncomfortable breast fullness, plugged ducts, or mastitis (breast infection).

77

Effects of Alternating Breast and Bottle

Alternating breast and bottle may seem the perfect solution, but it actually combines the disadvantages of both feeding methods. Early weaning from the breast is common because *alternating routines* lowers milk production, increases the amount of nipple confusion, and creates too much work for most mothers. However, certain forms of alternating feeding methods work well for triplets and other higher-order multiples.

Alternation generally takes one of two forms *with twins*: (1) breastfeed one twin and supplement the other at each feeding or (2) breastfeed both twins for one feeding and supplement both at the next. With either routine, a mother is investing the time and effort required for full breastfeeding and full bottle-feeding! If using infant formula, which takes longer to digest, babies actually may be missing more than every other breast-feeding so milk production can drop faster. An alternating routine is more likely to work if a mother: (1) has a helper to give bottles and handle the preparation and clean-up of bottle feeding; (2) uses a hospital-grade electric breast pump to increase or maintain milk production; and (3) breastfeeds each baby *at least* four times in 24 hours for a minimum total of eight breastfeedings.

Alternating feeding methods seems to work better for *higher-order multiples*. The increased likelihood that helpers will be available to prepare, feed a baby or two, and clean-up after bottle-feeding may help. Also, fewer breastfeedings are missed as it is more likely that at least one baby will be put to breast for all, or most, feedings. Mothers tend to rotate which one(s) are breastfed and which are bottle-fed for alternate feedings.

Breast-milk Feeding

Some mothers continue to pump their milk and breast-milk feed one or more multiples for weeks or months. Sometimes the situation results in one or all multiples never, or rarely, being put to breast; sometimes a mother chooses to breast-milk feed rather than breastfeed. Most often a mother feels overwhelmed by working with three or more preterm multiples who are small and have ongoing sucking difficulties after NICU discharge.

Breast-milk feeding has its advantages and disadvantages. Without a doubt, a mother's own milk is the best food for her infants, and her expressed milk contains antibodies to protect babies against many illnesses. Still, breast-milk feeding is not the same as direct breastfeeding, since it doesn't require mother's presence and feedings are important opportunities to get to know each baby. Also, direct breastfeeding is associated with optimal anti-infective properties transfer.

Fully breastfeeding any multiple and bottle-feeding the other(s), even when a baby receives only mother's milk in the bottle, should be avoided if possible, as it can affect a mother's relationship with each baby. Sometimes a mother fully breastfeeds one, but lack of time and an ongoing sucking difficulty mean that another is put to breast only when possible. When a birth complication or a physical defect has an ongoing effect on one baby's ability to effectively breastfeed, even "practice" breastfeeding may not be possible for one. In these instances a mother will want to feed the affected multiple as often as possible and increase other forms of skin contact with this baby.

Successful Breastfeeding

Full breastfeeding is nature's ideal, but breastfeeding does not have to be all or nothing. Modern breast pumps allow mothers of multiples to provide breast milk for their babies when full breastfeeding isn't possible or desired. Infant formula was originally manufactured for special infant feeding situations, and caring for multiples definitely falls in that category.

Although many mothers fully breastfeed twins, and some fully breastfeed triplets or quadruplets for several weeks to months, every family situation is unique. You and each of your multiples benefit no matter what the amount or duration of your shared breastfeeding experience.

19

DETERMINING
ZYGOSITY

T he cell formed by the fertilization of a female ovum (egg) by a male sperm is called the zygote. When referring to the individuals comprising a multiple-birth set, *zygosity* refers to the origin of fraternal multiples as two or more separate zygotes from conception or to identical multiples produced when a single zygote splits. The term *twin type* also may be used for zygosity, even when referring to higher-order multiples. (See Key 1.)

There are physical and emotional reasons for wanting to know whether multiples are identical or fraternal. Zygosity is as much a part of each multiple as their individual features, growth patterns, behavioral styles, and so on. Health may be affected by zygosity, which plays a role in treating certain conditions.

Evidence of Zygosity

Sometimes the determination of zygosity is straightforward. Parents and health professionals know multiples are *fraternal* when two are of different genders, each has a different blood type, or the babies' have completely different hair colors. When examination of the placenta reveals a single chorion, parents and professionals are then certain that the two babies sharing that membrane (and placenta) are *identical*.

It is not always possible to determine zygosity on appearances alone. Some informal surveys have indicated that 15 to 25 percent of parents aren't certain whether their multiples are fraternal or identical. Many were given a diagnosis of zygosity at the babies' birth, but they later doubted the classification.

Factors used to determine zygosity may not be accurate. The size and shape of multiples' heads, their weights, their lengths, and their skin tones at birth do not indicate zygosity. Multiples' later growth and development may be affected by pregnancy-related issues, so these are not always reliable indicators. No two multiples experience the exact same conditions in the womb, and exposure to somewhat different environments during pregnancy, labor, and birth, and in the newborn period can be responsible for short- and long-term differences in multiples of either zygosity.

If unsure if multiples are identical (monozygotic) or fraternal (dizygotic/polyzygotic), look for additional physical evidence as they grow. Identical (monozygotic) multiples have the same

- gender
- blood type and subtypes
- eye color
- hair color, texture, and general distribution
- facial features and ear shape
- body build

They also often develop similar mannerisms. Their patterns of physical and mental growth and development tend to be quite close, unless any was affected by a pregnancy or birth-related factor. No matter how much the children in a family resemble one another, they still demonstrate much more variation in their appearances, growth, and development (at comparable ages) when compared to monozygotic siblings.

Another clue is other people's reactions. Identical multiples frequently are confused by friends and relatives. Parents of identical multiples may have more difficulty telling babies apart when they are asleep, although they easily know one from the other(s) when they are awake. Without their personalities enlivening their features, identical multiples often look more alike.

Scientific Determination of Zygosity

When physical evidence isn't enough, accurate laboratory tests are available to determine zygosity. These include blood subtyping and genetic (DNA) testing. When most people discuss blood type, they generally are referring to the major blood types—A, B, or O. Each person also has many subtypes. Fraternal multiples may share the same major type and the Rh (rhesus) factor, but differences become apparent when blood is tested for subtypes. The increasing accessibility of genetic (DNA) testing has decreased the use of blood subtyping as a method for determining zygosity.

Genetic testing looks at areas of DNA (deoxyribonucleic acid), the hereditary material in cells, for the repeat of specific components. Everyone's DNA exhibits repeating areas, but the pattern of repeats is different from person to person, except for identical multiples. Scientists can be 99 percent certain of zygosity when comparing DNA for the "repeat" pattern of same-sex multiples.

Genetic (DNA) testing is the most reliable way to determine zygosity. Until recently, the high cost of testing created an impediment. Also, older tests required a blood sample from each child, and some parents did not wish to subject their children to this.

Newer testing methods are inexpensive and as accurate as the older ones. Yet they are so easy that parents can now order kits to get samples of their multiples' DNA at home. The mail-order method involves swabbing the inside of each multiple's cheek to remove cells for testing. (All cells contain DNA.) The swabs are then placed in the special solution sent with the kit, returned to the lab in a designated envelope, and analyzed. Parents receive a written report several weeks later. (See Appendix B: Resources—Zygosity Testing, for laboratories providing this service.)

The Need to Know

Zygosity, being an identical or fraternal multiple, is a part of identity—a significant aspect of who each child is. Parents should not let anyone tell them that knowledge of zygosity is unimportant. If a parent or any multiple wants to know, then it is important.

20

GETTING TO KNOW
YOUR BABIES

The word "bonding" has become synonymous with the idea of some sort of an "instant glue" that mysteriously cements parent and newborn during a magical moment soon after birth. Bonding actually refers to the formation of an enduring attachment between parent and baby. This ongoing process of "falling in love" with an infant begins during pregnancy and continues after birth. Humans were designed to fall in love with only one person at a time and, usually, a parent has only one infant to fall in love with. A parent of multiples *must* fall in love with two, three, or more persons at once.

A parent's interactions with the individual multiples create the foundation for each baby's sense of self. The process of attachment is intricately woven with the formation of a separate identity for each multiple. As a parent develops a strong, healthy attachment with each baby, that parent cannot help but get to know and treat multiples as individuals. Young multiples begin to realize during the toddler or preschool years whether each is loved and held in esteem as an individual or whether they are valued more as part of a set.

A Different Process
Learning to love two babies simultaneously is quite a different process from bonding with a single infant, and the process only becomes more complex as the number of multiples in a set increases. Forming a strong, separate attachment with each multiple takes months, or even years, longer than it does for a parent with a single baby.

There are many reasons for the longer attachment process, and several factors often complicate it. The early, extended contact with babies that enhances initial feelings of attachment is less likely to occur after a multiple birth. Prematurity and other complications of multiple pregnancy and birth often lead to parent-infant(s) separation and less opportunity for early close contact. Even when birth and early postpartum conditions are ideal, it can be difficult to relate to each baby separately.

During pregnancy, expectant parents imagine themselves caring for their baby after the birth, but the baby of prenatal daydreams is a fantasy baby. The fantasy baby is reconciled with the "real" baby when forming an attachment with a single infant.

Prenatal fantasies are multiplied when expecting multiple babies. Consider your prenatal fantasy life. Did you see your babies as fraternal or identical multiples? Did you envision same-sex multiples and were all a particular sex? Or were boy-girl multiples more appealing? How alike or different were your babies' appearances and temperaments in prebirth fantasies? Perhaps you visualized life with multiple easygoing, placid babies only to find yourself with ones having minds of their own.

Getting to know and accept the different and complicated little persons you actually gave birth to, rather than the ones you imagined, takes time. Yet time, or the lack of it, is a major factor in a prolonged attachment process. Quiet periods to enjoy one baby alone can be few and far between. It is also easy to miss opportunities to seize a few minutes with only one multiple when riding a dizzying baby care merry-go-round.

Considerations

Forming a separate attachment with each multiple is critical for the parent and the individual babies no matter how prolonged the process. Each multiple's physical and emotional health and well-being hinges on the development of an enduring attachment with parents. The twin-twin relationship, or the distinct relationships among higher-order multiples, can never replace each parent-child relationship.

Besides each multiple's need for a relationship with parents, each parent also needs to feel a deep bond with each child. After all, the relationships established with the children are the true rewards of child rearing.

Most parents do form a strong, separate attachment with each baby, so relax. Do not worry that you and your multiples must go through life without bonding if

- you happen to miss the early, extended contact
- you were separated from one or more after birth
- since hospital discharge, you have little time to interact with each baby separately.

Don't ignore any concern you might have about bonding with one or more, but give yourself and your babies time to get to know one another.

21

∧∧∧

FORMING
ATTACHMENTS

T he process of forming attachments with multiple infants can begin in different ways. A parent might develop a close feeling for one baby before the other(s). Sometimes a parent's closer feelings for a particular baby persist; sometimes a parent's closer feeling for one multiple alternates between or among the babies. For some parents, the initial attachment is for the multiple infants as a unit. They form a group bond before developing an attachment with the individual multiples.

Preferential Attachment

Certain situations are conducive to bonding more closely with one baby than the other(s). A parent is more likely to feel an initial closeness to the multiple who first responds, or interacts, with the parent or the one who is first in that parent's care. Forming a preference for a particular multiple seems to occur more often when one preterm or ill baby is able to make visual contact with the parent earlier than the other(s), one baby can be cared for by mother in her hospital room while the other(s) is separated from her in the NICU, or one is discharged from the NICU before the other(s). (See Key 47.)

- Often the multiple able to respond first and the one first in the parent's care is the same baby.
- Mothers are more likely to report that they quickly became attached to the baby constantly in their care, but fathers often spend more time with initially and feel closer to a baby in the NICU.

- Occasionally, a separated parent feels a psychic bond with a baby in the NICU and begins to form a closer attachment with the multiple not in her care.

- A first-born twin or triplet is more likely to receive preferential treatment. A second-born multiple (and third of triplets) is more likely to be affected by complications requiring special care, which may contribute to a preferential attachment with the first-born.

- Although ultrasound has greatly decreased the number of unexpected "bonus" babies, there continue to be sets of twins that are undiagnosed until labor or birth. One mother describing her unanticipated twin birth said, "For a long time I thought of the firstborn twin as 'my' baby. She was the baby I'd imagined during pregnancy. It was quite a while before I could think of the second-born 'surprise' as anything other than an intruder."

- Sometimes a parent feels closer to the "underdog" baby, the multiple that others are less attracted to for some reason. The underdog often is the baby who demands more attention, so the parent is forced to take time to interact with that baby. Chances are this is because the parent has had more opportunity to get to know and appreciate this baby's special qualities.

- Sets of boy-girl multiples may present a special circumstance. If a baby of specific gender was preferred, a parent may be naturally drawn toward and interact more with the one(s) of the desired gender. In this situation an initial NICU separation may cause feelings to be exaggerated or diminished, depending on which baby of what gender was more responsive, or in the parent's care, first.

- If one is born with some type of physical condition or a disability, a parent's feelings may be unequal. Again, a "perfect" baby is also the one more likely to be more responsive and in the parent's care first, which may influence feelings of attachment. (See Key 47.)

- Sometimes a parent simply experiences a better "fit" with one baby. This is more common with fraternal twins, because their temperaments tend to be more different.

Because an ongoing preference for any, but not all, of the multiples in a set can be devastating for every member of a family, it is important to recognize it and begin to work on a relationship with the multiple(s) to whom a parent feels less close. (See Key 23 for suggestions.)

Alternating Attachment

Sometimes a parent feels closer to one multiple, but within several weeks that feeling of closeness shifts to another baby. When a parent's focus and feelings of closeness shift from one baby to another (and back again) every few weeks, there is *alternating attachment*.

Some parents find their feelings and focus of attention alternate between/among babies from the first day. Others may form an attachment for the unit of multiples first, but an alternating attachment follows as parents begin to form separate relationships with their multiples. When weeks go by without a shift in focus from one baby, preferential attachment would be suspected.

Unit Bonding

Unlike parents who first bond more with one multiple than the other(s), some feel close to and protective of the set of multiples as a unit before they form an attachment with the individuals within the set. *Unit bonding* is more likely to occur when a parent is able to hold and care for both twins or all triplets from birth.

Unit bonding tends to lead to unit thinking—considering multiples as a single entity. One parent described this phenomenon by saying, "It seems as if I have one baby who keeps me constantly busy, although my brain knows I have two babies and I can see two babies in front of me." Unit thinking might account for the desire to dress multiples alike, which essentially allows them to take on a single image.

Unit bonding is more likely to occur with identical multiples. Quite likely this is related more to their similar body rhythms than to their physical resemblance, since few parents have difficulty telling identical multiples apart.

To make the attachment process more interesting, young multiples often flip-flop, demonstrating certain behaviors to a greater or lesser degree just as a parent thinks she is getting to know their differing responses. This can create confusion when parents are trying to get to know their babies as individuals. Flip-flopping seems to be most common for identical multiples and it often occurs during swings in behavioral patterns. The more similar fraternal twins' temperaments (behavioral styles) are, the more likely they are to flip-flop. This flip-flopping is most common during multiples' first year, and it recurs less often as they grow.

The more multiples look and act differently, the less time it takes to recognize and form attachments with the individuals within a set of multiples. Parents usually break through unit thinking earlier and discover each baby's uniqueness when multiples are of different genders. Since opposite-sex multiples tend to be the most different in appearance and temperament, this seems a logical progression.

Overlap

Although a parent of multiples may identify the attachment process with her/his multiples as mostly fitting with one style, overlap is common. A parent may feel an initial closeness to one yet still find she/he emphasized the multiples' unit in certain circumstances. Unit bonding often gives way to an alternating attachment process, as a parent focuses attention on one for a period of time and then shifts that focus to another. Overlap is another reason that the attachment process takes more time with multiple infants.

In Any Case . . .

Each multiple deserves a special relationship with both parents no matter how the situation affects the attachment process. Understanding how the attachment process differs with multiples may provide a basis for improving the relationship with each child.

22

PROMOTING ATTACHMENT

Today is a good day for parents to begin strengthening the emotional bonds they have with multiples—no matter what the current age of their children. Good relationships do not simply "happen." The participants in any long-term relationships must work at it.

The relationship a parent has with each multiple should be examined frequently to consider whether it is as good as it could or should be. By becoming aware of how the attachment process differs with multiples, a parent may be able to step back and take an objective look at her/his interactions with each multiple. Parents of multiples have recommended the following ways to accomplish this.

- Listen to the way you refer to your multiples. Do you frequently refer to them as "the twins" ("the triplets," "the quads," etc.), "the boys," "the girls," "the boy(s) and the girl(s)," or simply "they" rather than by name? If so, you may be falling into *unit thinking.*
- Do you refer to only one (or two) by name and the other(s) by gender, such as "Trevor and the girl(s)," or do you find you often refer to one (or two) by name but refer to the other multiple(s) as "he," "she," "they," or even "it"? If you find this happening, ask whether *preferential attachment* could be interfering with developing strong bonds with all the babies.
- Do you find you tend to respond quickly to a particular multiple (or two) but feel less bothered when the other one(s) signals distress or the need for attention? This may be another sign of forming a preferential attachment.

- Is the developing relationship with each multiple taking a backseat to accomplishing daily child-care tasks? When parents are asked before birth why they want children, their responses usually center on forming a relationship with each child. However, it is easy for parents to lose sight of this after their multiples' birth when simply trying to get through 12 to 30 feedings, 20 to 40 diaper changes, 2 or more baths, and so on, every day!

Parents of multiples have found several ways to develop a deep bond with each child. All involve taking action through simple changes in the parent's behavior.

- Don't waste time feeling guilty about disparate feelings of attachment. Guilt is an unproductive expenditure of mental energy, and you need all your energy to care for your multiples. Instead, *congratulate yourself* for recognizing the problem and use your energy for more frequent interactions with any less-favored multiple.
- Make a concerted effort to *increase skin contact* with each baby through infant massage and by holding each, separately or two (or more) at once, as much as possible. Forming and maintaining an attachment between any two human beings is dependent on one-to-one close contact. Kangaroo care is not just for premies, and no child is ever too old for backrubs, hugs, and kisses.
- As a parent of multiples you may depend on infant equipment more than other parents, but frequently evaluate *infant equipment use* versus its overuse or abuse, which can greatly reduce parent-multiple interaction. The best equipment makes everyday life easier yet helps parents to enhance individual connections with multiples through contact. For instance, a parent might alternate holding one or two multiples in some type of baby carrier or sling, which leaves one or two hands free while a baby or two enjoys a snuggle. As far as most babies and young children are concerned, sitting in a rocking chair on a parent's lap beats any wind-up swing ever invented.
- Take advantage of feedings, diaper changes, bath time, and so on, to grab a few minutes of *one-to-one time* with each multiple. Use imagination to "seize the moment" as multiples grow.

91

- Once *eye contact* is established with a particular multiple, you are in fact alone with that child even when holding more than one in your arms. Talk to one baby and imitate her facial expressions and vocalizations for a few minutes. Then turn, establish eye contact with another multiple, and focus on that baby for a few minutes.

- You probably took a lot of time to choose your multiples' names, so *call each by name.* When making eye contact with any multiple, go out of your way to address that baby by name as you talk to him. This helps each multiple learn that a specific name is special and unique to him or her.

- *Respond to the individual* baby's or child's needs and not to the set of "twins" ("triplets," "quads," etc.). Trying to treat each one of multiples exactly the same is a strategy doomed to fail, because each multiple is an individual. Each has different needs, and each one's needs will change over time. If you sometimes fall into this type of unit thinking, ask yourself how you would likely respond if these children had been born a year apart. Chances are equality wouldn't have been a consideration. You wouldn't have to think twice about giving each child the kinds of attention each needed.

The emotional ties formed during infancy set the tone for a lifelong relationship with each child. As with all relationships, these relationships will continue to require a parent's commitment to them and an investment of the parent's time and energy. The reward is an enduring bond between parent and each multiple that becomes stronger as multiples grow.

23

~~~~~~

EARLY
DIFFERENTIATION

D ifferentiation is a process that occurs when parents consciously and unconsciously compare their multiples' differences and similarities. These comparisons help parents learn to distinguish their babies' individual behavioral styles, or individual approaches to life. Differentiation, bonding (forming an attachment) and individuality are closely linked. Looking for differences between, or among, newborn multiples is one way for parents to begin to get to know their babies as individuals. Zygosity, whether multiples are fraternal or identical, often influences this differentiation process.

Physical Differences

No two persons look exactly alike, not even identical multiples. There are *always* physical differences. These may be very obvious as with some fraternal sets or the differences may be more subtle, as with other fraternal sets and for most identical sets.

Most parents have little difficulty telling their identical multiples apart after the first days or weeks. Frequently, one will have a longer, thinner face while another's face is rounder. Often each identical multiple has a different look about the eyes. One sometimes has a birthmark that the other(s) does not have. It can be more difficult distinguishing identical multiples while they sleep because their personalities are not influencing their features.

Behavior

Temperament and its influence on behavior are, as with physical features, related to heredity. Each multiple's behavioral approach to events or situations and their eventual personalities are a combination of genetic temperament traits plus all the environmental factors that influence behavioral response. Newborns can no more control their behavioral styles than they can their eye color or facial features.

- Just as they look more alike, identical multiples tend to behave more alike. If one is calm and easygoing, the other is more likely to be calm and easygoing, but if one leans toward fussiness, the other probably will be a fussier baby, too. However, the degree to which each expresses temperament traits or exhibits a particular behavioral style will vary to some extent. Sometimes identical multiples seem to take turns or flip-flop when they express some traits. (See Key 21.)
- As with any siblings, fraternal multiples may have similar or very different behavioral styles. Parents sometimes worry unnecessarily when they compare an active, high-need baby with an observant, more placid multiple.
- The internal body clock governing sleep-wake cycles also has genetic components. Identical multiples tend to wake for feedings and sleep at about the same times; and fraternal multiples are more likely to exhibit wider variations. (If getting multiples on a similar "schedule" is important, many parents report less variation when two or more multiples share a bed, or co-bed, during their early weeks or months.)

Growth and Development

- Multiples' developmental timetables may be similar or quite different. Identical multiples tend to gain about the same amount of weight each month, grow a similar number of inches, and develop physical skills at a comparable rate, except when any has an underlying health issue. As with any siblings in a family, some fraternal multiples may grow or develop on a similar curve, but fraternal multiples also can vary widely within the normal range for growth and development.
- Parents often express concern when fraternal multiples vary widely in their growth patterns. Each may exhibit a normal pattern, but one simply inherited Uncle Bill's large muscular physique while another has Grandma's petite, wiry frame.

- Different patterns of development also may be confusing and, the more babies in the set, the more confusing it can be. When one baby often gazes at a colorful mobile for long periods of time while another signals loudly that he couldn't care less, a parent may be reminding herself frequently of the wide range in normal for development skills and behavioral styles!

Promoting Differentiation

The process of differentiation may be one more tool that helps parents develop a relationship with each unique individual within a set of multiples. As a parent you can easily enhance this process on even the busiest day.

- Ignore those who say, "Never compare twins (triplets, quads, etc.)." This advice is completely unrealistic and it's impossible for most parents to follow! Discovering multiples' differences naturally leads to making comparisons between, or among, them. Every parent compares her baby with other babies the same age. As long as a parent makes the distinction between comparison and labeling, there should be no problem. Comparisons are general and flexible; they change as children grow and change. Labels, such as calling them "the happy one," "the smart one," or "the moody one" can be rigid and they often stick long after they no longer apply.
- Look for physical differences whether multiples closely resemble one another or not. If they do closely resemble and you are uncertain who is who initially, devise a way to positively identify at least all but one. (One can be identified without a mark by process of elimination.) Polish a fingernail or toenail of one of twins. For identical triplets or quadruplets, use noticeably different colors of nail polish for each. Hospital identification bracelets can be left on, but take extra ones home to change them as babies grow.
- Note the babies' similarities as well as their differences. Identifying similarities is also part of the differentiation process.
- Since a lot of time and thought was given to choosing names for multiples, refer to each by name when making eye contact.
- Take photographs of multiples together *and* separately.

- Don't feel concerned for now if compelled to dress infant multiples alike. Consider dressing them in look-alike outfits of different colors or in different outfits of the same color. This strategy recognizes both the specialness of multiples and their separateness.

- Become familiar with the range of normal variation in infant/child growth and development. Read about child growth and development for each age group before multiples reach it. Refer to a child growth and development reference when one multiple masters a physical skill or reaches a developmental milestone before another. Learning about normal growth and development and its variations will also provide clues if any multiple is not following a typical growth and development curve, which is more common with multiples because of the large number affected by preterm birth and other complications.

- If multiples were preterm, they may achieve developmental milestones closer to the time of their original due date (born at 37 or more weeks gestation) than according to their actual birth date. Ask the babies' pediatric care provider about adjusting their growth and developmental timetables.

- Identify each multiple's strengths and nurture them. If any has a more difficult temperament, remember that babies cannot be "good" or "bad," nor do they choose to be challenging or easygoing. Every challenging quality has positive aspects, and challenging babies often are sensitive and bright. (See Key 33.)

Parents influence each multiple's inborn patterns of development, but they can't change it completely. Multiples have the greatest chance to achieve their individual potentials when all are exposed to a stimulating environment, introduced to a wide variety of experiences, and responded to as individuals.

Early differentiation—noticing and comparing multiples' differences and similarities—provides a "black and white" view of the members within the multiples set. It may provide a foundation for recognizing each multiple as a unique individual and eventually helps parents move beyond unit thinking. (See Keys 21, 22, and 24.)

24

~~~~~~

INDIVIDUALITY ISSUES

P arents play a fundamental role in the development of a relationship between, or among, multiples. For example, parents
decide whether multiples are addressed as individuals or as a
group. Initially, they choose the clothing their multiples wear and
the toys they play with. They make decisions about separating their
multiples or keeping them together. Whether such decisions are
made consciously or not, a parent's approach to raising multiples
will focus on either the set of multiples or the individuals within it.

Although a parent may emphasize one approach, most parents feel pulled toward the other from time to time. It is normal to
want to treat multiples as different yet the same, separate but
equal. A parent can claim to promote each child's individuality in
one breath while in the next breath she makes certain that everyone in the vicinity knows she has multiple-birth children.

The development of a multiples-rearing approach that centers
on individuality or on the set may be rooted in the parent-multiple-
infants attachment process. The parent-infant relationship is considered a child's primary relationship; even the multiple-multiple
relationship(s) cannot replace it. (See Keys 20, 21, and 22.) Because
of the importance of the parent-child relationship, a child who is
part of a multiple-birth set usually caters to the parent's desire to act
more as an individual or as part of a "whole." Multiples will go along
with the approach that gains each more parental attention.

Equal but Different

Many parents feel an almost fanatical desire to treat multiples equally. Dressing multiples alike and devoting equal time to
each may be more "equality-mania" than unit thinking.

Some parents are concerned that their multiples, or others, may think one multiple is loved more if all are not treated exactly the same. Also, when parenting tasks are multiplied, equal treatment may seem to contribute to an organized approach to childcare. The multiples themselves often compound the problem. About the time a parent is finally getting to know each multiple as an individual, they are likely to enter a phase when each feels jealous of the other(s) so all then demand equal treatment. If one has some toy or a parent's attention, the other(s) immediately wants it, too.

It helps to respond to each child separately rather than to the set as a whole. No parent is obligated to treat multiples equally, and it is unrealistic to try. Each multiple is a separate child, like any single-born child. Each has a different need for the parents' time and attention, and the needs will change as they grow. Few parents would hesitate to respond differently to siblings born a year apart. Multiples deserve the same kind of individualized response.

The Celebrity Syndrome (CS)

Our culture adores multiples and considers them special. Multiples become celebrities, commanding attention wherever they go. Their parents become celebrities and gain public attention simply by giving birth to more than one baby at a time. It can be fun to bask in the limelight. Let's face it, there are moments when the public's adulation may help a harried, sleep-deprived parent through the day. There is no reason to feel guilty for taking advantage of infant or toddler multiples' celebrity on occasion. In fact, parents may want to think of it as a coping mechanism!

Problems arise if perspective disappears and celebrity status is taken too seriously. When this occurs, the set of multiples is stressed at the expense of the individuals because parental celebrity status depends on multiples' specialness as a unit.

Beware. The celebrity syndrome can strike parents no matter what the age of their multiples. To decide whether you may be in danger of succumbing to the celebrity syndrome, give yourself CS points if you

- frequently refer to your children by their set name, such as "the twins," "the triplets," "the quads," and so on, rather than by their individual names—add points if other persons have followed your example and call them by their set name, and give yourself extra points if you frequently call your multiples "the twins" ("the triplets," "the quads," etc.) in front of them.
- ever boast you have difficulty telling two or more of the multiples apart—add points if you do this in front of them.
- often inform others that your little darling is part of a set when you are out with only one—add points if this is said within hearing range of the little darling.
- encourage the wearing of look-alike outfits, including look-alike outfits in different colors—add CS points if you change all outfits to keep them looking the same when only one is dirty, and add extra points if multiples are older than toddlers and could help select their own clothing each day.

A high score does not necessarily mean you have been seduced by the celebrity syndrome, but it does indicate the time has come to ask yourself why you seem to be treating your multiples as a unit. Does this emphasis benefit them or you?

Resolving Individuality Issues

Once a parent truly gets to know each multiple, it is impossible to treat them as anything other than individuals. Concerns commonly related to multiple-birth children, such as how to dress them or when to separate them become meaningless. Such decisions then are based on each child's current needs. They are not arbitrarily determined by the entire "set" or group.

The temptation to enjoy celebrity status and the desire to give multiples equal time and attention do not completely disappear as they grow. When a parent concentrates on the relationship with each multiple, the word *multiple* (twin, triplet, quad, etc.) alone soon becomes a poor definition for any child. At the same time, multiples will be developing the relationship(s) with the other member(s) of the set, and a parent then begins to see what a special part that plays in the development of each of them.

25

~~~~~~

HOW OTHERS VIEW YOUR MULTIPLES

Parents set the tone for how relatives and friends view multiples. If others are encouraged to see them as individuals instead of as a unit, they probably will. Other people may need a subtle nudge in the right direction, but with a little guidance parents usually can secure their cooperation.

If you call your children "the twins," "the triplets," or "the quads," others will probably do the same. Call each of your babies by name, and ask others to do likewise. If someone forgets, restate your preference. Something such as, "We prefer that you call them Mark, Sarah, and Andrew, since they are separate persons," will do. Remind persistent resistors, but avoid long or irritated dissertations on why this is necessary.

Parties and Gifts

Parents may have to tell well-meaning friends and relatives to give separate cards and gifts for birthdays and holidays. Explain how joint gifts and cards make children feel lumped together. Let them know that multiples usually prefer separate inexpensive gifts unless it is something really big, easily shared or used at the same time, and wanted by all.

When it's time for birthday parties, parents sometimes have a separate party for each child or one big party to which each multiple is encouraged to invite his or her own guests. It is up to parents to take the initiative as to how they want these situations handled. If guests' parents aren't asked to send a gift only for the multiple who invited their child, some will send gifts for each multiple and other parents only for one. An unequal number of gifts often creates hurt feelings for any multiple with fewer gifts.

You, the Celebrity

Parents become celebrities when multiples are born. Strangers often feel free to invade a family's privacy, referring to multiples in the third person even in their presence. Others may presume familiarity and sometimes ask personal and embarrassing questions, and they have been known to make ridiculous and even insulting comments!

Parents may as well forgive these offenses as part of human nature, but it doesn't hurt to be prepared to handle invasions of privacy. The more babies in a set, the more curious everyone is likely to be, but parents' first responsibility is to their babies. You don't "owe" the public anything.

- You may resent positive *and* negative comments, such as "double trouble," or "quintuple blessing," which minimize the situation by reducing this complex and intense experience to something trivial. You could respond with the opposite phrase, either positive or negative, regardless of feelings at that moment, or say nothing.
- Expect questions about your fertility and how the multiples were conceived, but do not think you have to respond with anything but a polite, "Why do you ask?" or "Don't you think that's rather personal?" This throws the question back at the questioner.
- Some people feel that if they compliment one baby it is OK to insult the other(s). How can a parent respond when someone says, "She has such beautiful blue eyes. Isn't it a shame the other one(s) eyes are hazel?" Simply say, "We like hazel, too."
- You may have to deal with preconceived labels, such as one baby is "good," another one is "bad," one is "cranky" and another one is "happy."
- The public can be extremely insensitive to the feelings of a disabled child. When one or more of multiples has a disability, don't feel you must respond to rude remarks. It's OK to just glare and move on if someone is rude.

- When you have multiples, many people assume that your family is complete. This is especially true if you have at least one child of each gender. What is a parent supposed to say when someone approaches with the comment, "How wonderful. You got it all over with at once!"? Having more children or not is a couple's choice, and it is not necessary to defend the decision. Again, answer a question with a question, for instance, "Why would you say that?" or respond with a "maybe" and a mysterious look.
- On a cheerier note, there are certain advantages to this newly found celebrity status. People often tolerate incredibly rambunctious behavior from multiples that would not be tolerated from a single child. When older multiples are likely to make a public spectacle, dress them alike and accept others' patient understanding as your due!

Teachers

Older multiples are likely to spend a great deal of time away from home and in school, and teachers can have a tremendous influence on how multiples view themselves. Teachers should follow the parents' lead. Schedule separate conferences for each child, and unless the discussion centers on something that concerns their relationship, do not mention the other(s). Watch for indications that faculty and staff are confusing them. This sometimes happens even when multiples are separated. One mother scheduled a conference to discuss one twin's feelings of inadequacy, only to be told that he had received numerous honors during the year. When she asked for a list of these awards, teachers realized it was his twin who had received every one. (See Key 45.)

Self-image

You can only control your own views and how you treat your multiple children. If, despite your best efforts, others continue to treat your twins as a unit, it should not have a devastating effect. The clearest picture they have of themselves comes from their parents. The strong self-image you help establish during their childhoods should carry them through.

26

~~~~~~

NEW MOTHER
FEELINGS

The babies have finally arrived, and you may be surprised if feelings of excitement and elation are mixed with feelings of anxiety and apprehension. What you actually feel and what you think you *should* feel may conflict. Many factors may have an impact on a mother's early feelings about her babies and motherhood times two or more. Was the babies' birth extremely premature? Was the labor and birth all you expected and hoped for, or was an emergency cesarean or other unanticipated birth intervention necessary? Have you received the physical and emotional support you've needed from others?

The physical changes occurring during the first weeks or months after a multiple birth can wreak havoc with maternal emotions. The new mother's postpartum body hasn't returned to "normal," and it may seem as though it never will. The center of attention shifts from the expectant mother to her newborn babies. The responsibility of caring for multiple newborns may seem overwhelming, yet many new mothers find it difficult to ask others for help. Some mothers feel a heightened sense of possessiveness for their babies, others feel distant or detached, and some find their feelings see-sawing in both directions.

Recovery

Recovering from multiple pregnancy and birth often takes longer than recovery after a single pregnancy and birth. The most ideal multiple pregnancy is more physically stressful than a single pregnancy, but multiple pregnancy also is more often associated with complications. Strict forms of bed rest during pregnancy, the aftereffects of certain complications, surgical birth, and excessive blood loss or actual postpartum hemorrhage may affect a new mother's physical and emotional health. All may contribute to physical weakness and fatigue, and feeling "blue" or overwhelmed at times. Many experts recommend physical therapy (PT) or special reconditioning programs to help a woman regain fitness after coping with complications or spending weeks on bed rest.

In addition to physical recovery, new mothers of multiples may worry when their bodies don't return to "normal" shapes and sizes within a few weeks of birth. A few "holdover" pounds (kilos), stretch marks, and loose abdominal skin can affect body image. Many wonder if their husbands find them attractive. However, it is unrealistic to expect a quick return to prepregnancy size and shape when several months were required to get out of shape. A new mother of multiples should give herself months to get back in shape. Exercise, such as pushing a multiple stroller filled with babies, and wearing clothing to camouflage any bulges, often helps as the body slowly returns to its former proportions.

A new mother of multiples does not have the luxury of focusing only on herself and her personal needs as she recovers. Instead, recovery must be accomplished as she assumes care for a greatly expanded family. Many mothers have unrealistic expectations about newborn babies' abilities or about their ability to care for multiples without help. As a result, some mothers become anxious about caring for two or more babies. Some mothers also feel as if no one understands what they are dealing with. Eventually, they feel isolated and cut off from others.

The physical and mental changes that follow multiple pregnancy and birth may contribute to the higher number of mothers of multiples affected by *postpartum depression* and *anxiety disorders*. More than 20 to 25 percent of mothers of multiples experience postpartum depression at some time during their babies' first two years compared with about 10 percent of mothers of single infants. This number does not reflect those affected by postpartum anxiety or adjustment disorders. Also, a *postpartum post-traumatic stress disorder* has been identified among some women who were on strict or prolonged bed rest during pregnancy.

Depression and other postpartum mental or emotional disorders don't just affect the postpartum woman. They have a profound effect on the babies, other children, and spouse. Fortunately, these disorders are extremely treatable *when* a woman doesn't ignore symptoms and seeks help from an appropriate health professional. Contact your health-care provider immediately if you *frequently*

- have little or no appetite or never stop eating
- have difficulty sleeping even when babies are asleep
- feel "foggy" and can't concentrate or make decisions
- become teary or lose emotional control
- feel emotionally detached from your babies and others
- feel panicky sensations along with difficulty breathing, dizziness, or faintness, and/or alternating hot flushes and chills
- wonder if you are depressed or overanxious.

Household Routine

Most humans crave predictable patterns in their lives. Continuity provides reassurance and comfort. The birth of multiples necessitates the development of an entirely new pattern or routine. Until a new pattern emerges and becomes the daily routine, new parents may feel disoriented and unsure of themselves. There is no set time frame for a new routine to develop, but it generally takes several months. Don't worry if a lack of routine results in feelings of ambivalence, and don't compare your situation with any family that recently added only one baby to their household.

Many new mothers experience tremendous highs and lows as they learn to care for and get to know their babies. Whether they are in the midst of a high or a low often depends on to what degree a routine has evolved and how reliable any sort of routine has become. On days when everything goes according to plan, a new mother may feel superior and the luckiest woman alive to have her babies. On days when nothing seems to be working, a mother may feel inadequate and out of control, and wonder why she had to be the one to have two, three, or more babies at once.

Whether a routine has emerged or not, you are likely to feel better if you *make* a little time for yourself each day. It is more energizing to spend this time doing something you enjoy rather than something you think you should be doing. Snatching little bits of time may be all that is realistic for now, but little bits add up.

Mothering Style

New mothers tend to be vulnerable to others' comments or opinions about parenting style. You are unique as a mother and each of your multiples also is unique. You and each baby will develop a relationship that is different than every other mother-child relationship. Try not to take relatives', friends', or parenting book authors' comments or opinions personally. Thank concerned or interested persons for their thoughts, but do as you think best for you and your children. Listen to each of your babies rather than depend on the comments of others. Trust what you read in each baby's behaviors rather than the generalized advice offered in books. Incorporate only the suggestions you think will be a good "fit" for your family.

Don't be surprised if you feel closer to one multiple than the other(s). There are a variety of reasons for unequal feelings. Don't deny unequal feelings if they exist, because denial interferes with forming a closer relationship with the other multiple(s). Instead, accept these feelings and then work through them until you've achieved a close relationship with each multiple. (See Key 23.)

The reality of caring for multiple newborns may be accompanied by feelings of apprehension and anxiety. However, most new mothers also experience intense emotions of wonder, joy, and excitement when they look upon their babies lying side by side. Feelings of anxiety and apprehension tend to fade as you become more confident of your ability to mother multiples, but the feeling of awe rarely fades no matter what your multiples' age.

27

~~~~~~

FATHER FEELINGS

Surveys indicate that after the initial shock and excitement of the discovery of a multiple pregnancy, expectant fathers often worry about increased financial obligations. As his wife's pregnancy progresses a father may feel anxious about the health of his wife and babies.

Becoming involved is the best way to gain reassurance. Accompany your wife to the obstetric care provider visits and for her sonograms. Ask questions. Be supportive. She is concerned, too, and usually will appreciate your involvement.

Bonding begins as soon as a father learns he is having twins, triplets, or more. Try to visualize your new babies. Begin to let the reality of multiple babies set in.

Your wife and any older child need your attention, help, and support both during this pregnancy and after the babies are born. Your wife will not be able to keep up her prepregnancy pace. Offer to take over some of her responsibilities. Pay extra attention to an older child, so he or she will not feel left out.

Fathers sometimes expect life to return to normal shortly after the babies arrive. A new "normal" life emerges, but it cannot be what it was before. Your family has expanded by more than the customary one, and it is going to be different. In the long run, it is better, but it takes time to adjust. (See Key 31.)

Fathers of multiples usually have to take a more active role in infant care than they would with a single baby. Extra hands to lavish love and attention on babies are always needed! Most view this as a very positive experience.

"One of the nicest things about having triplets," said one father, "is knowing they need *me* to care for them, too. My wife could handle our single infant by herself."

Most mothers develop an organized system to cope with multiples. It will not include you if you are not home much. If this happens, insert yourself into her plan whenever you are available. Do not wait for your wife to ask for help. It is not that your wife consciously leaves you out, she simply has learned to cope and needs a reminder when you are there.

Having multiples gives you a fantastic opportunity to stretch your role as a father. For instance, older children need reassurance that they are important. Their need for attention increases while their mother's time for them decreases. At the same time, each baby needs as much cuddling as a single baby. You, their father, can provide the extra arms for loving, cuddling, feeding, bathing, rocking, and walking.

Be the one to tie up loose household ends. Your wife will appreciate help with any kind of housekeeping. Take over a number of routine chores, such as grocery shopping or the laundry. The important thing is that you take over not only the actual task, but also the responsibility for completing it.

The lives of other new parents may seem to return to normal long before yours. Do not be discouraged. They are only making the adjustment to the birth of one baby. You and your family are adjusting to more. It is a wonderful and unique, but abnormal, situation. Those with "normal situations" never experience the thrill of watching multiples grow up.

28

~~~~~~

FINDING TIME TO BE A COUPLE

The birth of multiples changes the dynamics of a family. Many couples are unprepared for the changes within their relationship that accompany the birth of more than one baby at once. Everyone responds to change, stress, lack of sleep, and possibly inadequate nutrition in a unique way and it is difficult to plan a response to this situation.

One very important dynamic for any family is the relationship between mother and father. In all your planning for multiples, it is easy to ignore yourselves as a couple. You may think that this "couple" relationship will miraculously return to "normal" within a few weeks of the babies' birth, but this is usually an unrealistic expectation.

Getting to know and care for more than one baby requires a tremendous amount of time, which can be physically and emotionally all-consuming for both parents. So much is happening every day that the couple relationship may seem lost in the shuffle. Fathers generally become aware of this loss sooner than mothers because their bodies and emotions have not been upset by pregnancy and birth and fewer fathers are the primary caregiver.

Keep the following in mind when evaluating where you think you and your spouse are in your relationship. These tips may help place any negative feelings into perspective:

- It takes a mother longer to recover from multiple pregnancy and childbirth. This is especially true when a woman has a cesarean (surgical) delivery. (Fathers, see Key 26.)
- A mother who spends all day caring for babies and young children, even if she has help, often feels "touched out." She is in physical contact with at least one other human for most or all of the day and she may not feel up to more contact or lovemaking with her spouse at the end of the day.
- Men's physical drives and needs change little with the birth of multiples. Their bodies have not gone through huge changes. They return to work and in a short period of time have more of an accustomed daily routine.
- Many husbands have an intense need to interact and make love to their wives as they did before their babies' birth. Both partners must compromise to meet each other's physical and emotional needs. For example, making love on the same timetable and with the same abandon as before the babies were born is unrealistic, but making an appointment for a brief romantic interlude during a nap period may be an option.
- Physical and emotional needs differ from individual to individual and from couple to couple. Do not compare each other or yourselves as a couple with anyone else. Do what is right for you.

Communication is the key to a happy marriage after the birth of multiples. Each parent must make his or her needs known to the other. Don't expect the other to "know" what is needed. Your time is limited, so be creative in showing your partner that he or she is still important. The following suggestions have been used by other parents of multiples.

- Say, "I love you," often. This takes no energy and can be said anytime.
- Go out of your way once each day to do something considerate for the other. One new mother woke her husband every day and gave him his morning coffee and paper in bed. No matter what happened the rest of the day, he felt loved. He took charge of washing the diapers. This may sound less romantic, but she said

that his performing that thankless chore was a definite affirmation of his love for her.

- Assume nothing. Say what you mean in a nonthreatening way. Tell your spouse how you feel. Each of you may be too tired or too busy to pick up on nonverbal communications.
- Take walks together, or eat dinner by candlelight even if each of you holds a baby or two.
- Make dates with each other, and look forward to the time you spend together.
- Give each other time away alone. Agree to be the one to get up with the babies during the night to ensure that your partner gets several hours of uninterrupted sleep. Mothers especially may appreciate these considerations.
- Be creative with lovemaking. Forget past notions of the proper time or place. Exhausted parents are rarely in the mood late in the evening. Make an appointment with each other for early in the morning, or hire a sitter to take the children for a walk.

New parents often wonder if there is life after having multiples. They seem all-consuming at first, but there is definitely life after multiples and it can be even more special when you are sensitive to one another.

29

SIBLING ADJUSTMENT

Look at life for the family of newborn multiples from the perspective of an older sibling. Not one baby, but two or more even have come to displace her as the center of her mother's and father's world. Relatives and friends visit, and in their haste to see the babies, they often ignore her. Strangers on the street inch her aside to ogle multiple babies in a stroller. People used to tell her *she* was beautiful; now they tell her how lucky she is to have so many babies.

She is not feeling lucky. Babies cry a lot. Her mother is always tired. Just when she has her mother's undivided attention, a baby needs to be fed or changed. Instead of reading her a story when he comes home from work, her father cares for the babies so her mother can get dinner on the table. "Wait a minute" suddenly becomes her parents' favorite response to any request.

Parents want and need to nurture all their children, not only the multiples. Coming home with more than one baby does not change the needs of older children. Fortunately, there are ways to ensure their position as important members of the family. These suggestions may be helpful in dealing with an older child:

- Acknowledge the older child's negative feelings. Let him know you understand his frustrations.
- Talk to older children about when they were babies. Tell them how much time was spent taking care of them. Show them photos and videotapes of themselves as babies.
- The special treatment multiples may receive from others rarely extends to other children. Explain to your older children that

multiple babies take extra time and attention. It is not that multiples are more special.

- Spend some uninterrupted time with any older child each day. You might arrange to do this during the babies' nap time, or hire a baby-sitter to take the babies for a walk.

- *Regression* (acting younger by wetting pants or "forgetting" a skill) can be a child's natural reaction to a dramatic change in routine. Do not make a big deal of it, but emphasize the privileges of being a "big kid."

- You may not be able to control strangers, but you can direct friends and relatives to pay attention to your older children.

- When you go out with an older child and multiples, try to call as little attention to the "parade" as possible. The more children in a family the less easy this is, but try allowing an older child to ride in the multiple stroller while you carry an infant in a sling, soft carrier, or back pack. This makes the sibling feel special and you are less likely to be stopped by strangers.

- Help children appreciate their place within the family structure as older siblings. Fathers often have more time to spend with older children doing fun things.

- Mention occasionally that you appreciate the time that you and each child spend together. You might also point out that you and they can do certain things together because they are older.

- Have realistic expectations of older children. You sometimes may be so desperate for help that even the youngest older sibling is seen as a kind of mother's helper. Older children's interest in helping with babies will vary. Some love it, but others are apathetic. Also, children have short attention spans.

- Encourage a positive relationship between older siblings and the babies who have disrupted their lives. Don't "blame" the birth of the multiples for everything you can no longer do. If you used to go to the pool every day but can only make it once a week now, your older children do not need to be reminded that the babies are the reason.

- Let older children, even toddlers, know that you sometimes feel overwhelmed with all there is to do. They appreciate knowing your feelings and that you are human, too.

- When your babies reach the toddler stage, expect new feelings of frustration from older children. Once twins are mobile, they disturb their siblings' life-style because toddlers, by nature, get into everything. Older children, by nature, do not put their things away! Give older children their own space. Place sliding locks on the bedroom doors, so their things are safe from toddlers.

Each of your children will react to the birth of multiples in a different way. Some siblings seem to bask in the glow of the family's notoriety at first, but may express resentment later. As parents you need to be aware of possible negative feelings and prepare yourself to deal with them as part of a natural growth process.

Siblings often differentiate between multiples before their parents, often preferring one baby more than the other(s) at first. As they grow, most single siblings easily develop a separate relationship with each multiple.

If an older sibling appears to be bonding with only one of the multiples, encourage a relationship with each of the babies. Ask the older child to play with another while you care for the "favorite." Take short outings with the older sibling and another baby. "Notice" that another baby has a special smile just for that child.

Growth Experience

Siblings' lives change greatly with the birth of multiples. As they learn to do things on their own, they experience a growth in self-confidence. Each has a special place within the family unit, and parents have the responsibility of reaffirming the importance of this position.

30

CREATING A SUPPORT NETWORK

Sharing experiences and feelings with another person who is or already has waded through the early years with multiple-birth children can be tremendously supportive. Families with multiples are unique. They feel a special kind of joy and experience concerns that are associated only with multiples.

Mothers are particularly vulnerable to feeling alone and isolated. Generally, the mother provides the bulk of babies' care, and she is expected to maintain the sense of emotional well-being within a family. In today's culture, she quite likely has outside projects as well. It is difficult to carry out all these roles in a vacuum.

Fathers of multiples are expected to pitch in more than fathers of single newborns. Dad often helps any older child(ren) through the adjustment to two or more new brothers or sisters. A husband's/father's needs often take a back seat to those of the babies, any older child(ren), and the recuperating wife/mother.

The round-the-clock care multiples require can leave older child(ren) feeling displaced. They must deal with the loss of time and attention formerly lavished on them. If a more complicated pregnancy affected a mother's ability to care for older children, bringing home multiple babies is not going to ease the situation.

Creating a Network

A support network will not form out of thin air. Parents must create their own by searching for other parents and established groups that meet in person or on the Internet. Most parents prefer to speak to others having the same number of multiples in a set. Just as

115

parents of single-born children cannot really understand what it is like to add twins to a family, parents of twins cannot appreciate the additional complexities of triplets. Parents of quadruplets face issues that aren't as common for parents of triplets.

A new father may appreciate hearing another dad describe the effect having multiples has had on his marriage and family. Discussing the impact of multiples with other fathers may ease feelings of tension and help a father maintain perspective.

Older children also benefit from the understanding and camaraderie of a support system. Depending on their ages and moods, these children may share feelings of pride or frustration at the intrusion in their lives by multiple brothers and sisters. Sometimes older single-born children of different families "adopt" one another and form a pretend set of multiples!

Local organizations for parents of multiples often are listed in the white pages of the phone book. Chapters are listed on national organizations' Internet sites. Contact the public library or a local newspaper and ask if they have a listing of local organizations. In large urban areas, there may be a special group for parents of higher-order multiples. Major organizations can help parents locate groups or members living in nearby communities.

Attending parent meetings often leads to instant friendships. There is almost always another parent whose multiples are the same age and gender or who shares a similar parenting philosophy. Most groups hold monthly meetings and often invite guest speakers. Many groups include clothing and baby equipment sales, family get-togethers, and holiday celebrations.

A phone buddy is wonderful. When no local group exists or caring for multiples makes it difficult to attend meetings, consider the closest group as a resource. Contact the group representative to ask if another parent with a similar "multiples" situation could call or agree to be contacted.

The Internet has had an incredible impact on the ability to network with other parents of multiples. There now are numerous online discussion groups, including ones only for fathers. Some are sponsored through the major organizations for parents of twins and higher-order multiples. (See Appendix B: Resources.)

Obstetric, pediatric, and other health-care providers are sources of contact with local parents of multiples. Ask if they know other parents who would welcome a call, or give permission to share your name and number with another parent. Friends and relatives may know other parents. Everyone knows someone with multiples!

Of course, the multiples themselves are wonderful icebreakers. Two mothers became best friends after introducing themselves at a shopping mall as each pushed her twins in a double stroller. One mother knocked on a stranger's door after observing twins playing in the yard. They became immediate "best friends" and have maintained their friendship for more than 20 years.

Other Support Systems

Breastfeeding Support

If you are planning to breastfeed or are currently breastfeeding multiples, contact the mother support organization, La Leche League, in your area. Mothers can contact the international office by phone or via the web site for local leaders, leaders that have breastfed multiples, or non-U.S. leader contacts. La Leche League International also may have information about other breastfeeding support resources if in an area without an LLL group. (See Appendix B: Resources—Breastfeeding/Lactation.)

Mothers of multiples are more likely to need the support and services of a *lactation consultant*. Many hospitals now employ lactation consultants for their patients (mothers and babies) during the hospital stay and after discharge. There also are lactation consultants who work in the community. Health professionals who have been certified for this role will have the initials IBCLC (International Board Certified Lactation Consultant). Contact the hospital where you are to give birth and ask if lactation consultants will be available and whether they keep a roster of those in the community. (To locate an IBCLC in your area, see Appendix B: Resources—Breastfeeding/Lactation.)

Physical/Household Support

There are two forms of *doula* support. Some doulas provide support for women during *labor and birth*. Others support women, newborns, and their families after hospital discharge as *postpartum* doulas. Postpartum doulas can provide certain types of services in the home for a specified time period. Many doulas have education in breastfeeding support, and some "specialize" in families with multiple newborns. For information about certified doulas (CD) in your locale, see Appendix B: Resources—Birth and Postpartum Support: Doulas.

Other options for *babies' care* or *household help* include professional nanny or au pair providers and housecleaning services. Contacting agencies providing these services usually is easy via the phone book. Mothers have also found help with babies, any older child(ren), and housecleaning by posting positions on job boards at colleges, such as the boards for students in a college of education or nursing or on junior and senior high school boards.

Mental Health Support

The addition of multiples to a family has a tremendous impact on every member's life, and there may be a time when it isn't enough to speak with other families with multiples. Sometimes a family benefits from working with a counselor or a psychotherapist to discuss the effect multiples have had and develop additional coping skills. This can be particularly true when

- a new mother is affected by postpartum depression or another of the postpartum mental and behavioral disorders
- any family member exhibits persistent behavioral change indicative of difficulty adjusting
- either partner believes the marriage relationship is in jeopardy
- additional stressful events or situations are affecting a family

When any family member thinks professional help may be needed, it probably is.

Families with extra babies need extra support—both emotional and physical support. If parents are willing to seek it, a world full of support systems is waiting to help them!

31

~~~~~~

A "ROUTINE" ADJUSTMENT PERIOD

Expectant parents tend to idealize what life will be like with multiple newborns. The babies of pregnant daydreams eat and sleep on a predictable, synchronized, and convenient schedule that always allows for several hours of uninterrupted sleep at night. Daydream multiples rarely cry and are easily comforted. Holding two or more at once is not a problem in daydreams.

The mother in this fantasy quickly recovers from the physical changes of a multiple pregnancy and birth. Fatigue never touches her. This well-rested woman has plenty of patience as she lovingly cares for newborn multiples and the rest of her family. She soon figures out a way to accomplish household tasks, jump back into work-related projects, *and* fit into her prepregnancy clothing.

The dream husband always pitches in to help. He always knows exactly what needs to be done without having to ask. He is as willing and able to throw in loads of wash as he is to juggle two or more babies at once.

The fantasy family with newborn multiples is perfect. Real families adapting to two, three, four, or more newborns are not. This Key focuses on realistic expectations for the initial adjustment period after the babies' homecoming.

Getting Back to Normal

New parents often say they can't wait to "get back to normal," whether they are expecting a single infant or multiples. Anticipating only minimal disruption, they expect their new babies will soon fit into the predictable daily routine the household followed before the pregnancy. It is natural for parents of multiples to crave a "boring" but predictable routine after a pregnancy and birth that is more physically demanding at best and often fraught with complications and medical interventions at worst. However, it is unrealistic to believe it will occur.

The first few months of infancy are usually marked more by disruption of household routine than its restoration. Fitting multiple newborns into a family's life cannot help but add to the disruption. When this disruption is unexpected, it can leave new parents feeling confused and frustrated with the loss of control over daily events.

Unlike the body of prenatal fantasies, a woman's real postpartum body often feels tired, weak, and achy for several weeks after multiples are born. That postpartum body has been through a lot in a short time!

Babies have been through a lot in a short time, too, especially if preterm or affected by other complications. However, every newborn deals with amazing physical changes outside the womb and each baby has a unique response to "extra-uterine" life. Parents must figure out the differences in their multiple newborns' approaches to these life adaptations.

Real babies have not read the child-care book guidelines about infant schedules. They cannot understand that parents, especially their postpartum mother, could use more sleep instead of less. Real babies are incredibly immature humans and completely dependent on others. Is it any wonder then that parents sometimes become overwhelmed as they try to figure out and meet the needs of two or more different newborns when also working to meet their own important physical and emotional needs and those of other family members?

Fortunately, postpartum chaos is temporary! Although new parents can never return to their prepregnant routine, a "new normal" routine *will* develop. However, it will take time.

Discovering this new normal routine also requires more compromise on the parts of parents than babies, since parents are mature adults with two or more decades of life experience.

Influences on Routine

Multiples' inborn behavioral styles and parents' attempts to differentiate between, or among, the babies can affect new parents' perceptions of an evolving predictable routine. When busy caring for multiple newborns around the clock, parents may not realize that a daily routine is developing or they may feel compelled more than a parent of a single newborn to impose a more rigid routine on the babies and household. Generally, a fairly predictable daily routine emerges by about three months, whether parents work hard to develop a schedule or they simply take it one day at a time.

Concern about a growing dependence on household helpers sometimes contributes to the desire for a schedule. Having physical help with the babies and the household for long periods of time is more likely after a multiple birth, especially for triplets and other higher-order multiples. Many parents find it takes some getting used to having others frequently in their home. It is not always easy to have helpers rotating in and out day after day. A parent may feel both grateful for the help and resentful of the loss of privacy at times. They may regret missing the intimacy of caring for one's own child alone while also appreciating the extra hands that mean babies' needs are being met quickly. If a schedule is seen as the way to decrease dependence on others' help, it is no wonder some parents seem willing to do almost anything to create one.

Balance and *flexibility* are crucial components of any new schedule that includes young children: If too rigid, sticking to a schedule can become more important than connecting with the tiny human beings entrusted to one's care; if too loose, it may intensify parental feelings of being overwhelmed. Babies are not machines, and no two are alike in their need for contact and comfort. Each baby will have the need to connect with a parent at times that may not "fit" with the ideal schedule, and the number of times "nonscheduled" connections are requested is bound to multiply when there are multiple newborns.

Unfair Comparisons

Parents of multiples often compare their postpartum family with one that recently added a single newborn family member. The other family may seem to have drawn the loose ends together and developed a new routine weeks ago; meanwhile, the parents of multiple newborns remain in a state of confusion. It can be difficult for a parent of multiples to avoid the temptation to compare herself/himself and their family with others. Somehow, it is easy to forget that the parents of multiples have at least twice as many unique individuals to get to know and integrate into the family and their lifestyle as the average new parents.

It takes time to let go of an "old" routine and any prenatal fantasies. Give yourself, your spouse, and your children all the time it takes to find a new pattern for daily life. The "new normal" life of the family with multiples will eventually exceed the expectations of any fantasy. The multiple little persons that parents give birth to are always far more interesting than the children they might have thought they wanted in those prenatal daydreams.

32

~~~~~~

HOUSEHOLD
ORGANIZATION

*P*rioritizing tasks is key to any successful routine. Newborns must be the top priority. Babies cannot and should
not be put off. They have needs that must be met, which do
not change simply because they come as a set. Any organizational
system must meet their needs while also meeting your family's basic
needs.

Key issues for most parents are feeding babies and the rest of
the family, meeting sleep needs, doing the laundry, and keeping up
with housework. "Keep it simple" should be the motto. By doing
so, you "buy" time to spend caring for your babies.

Put the immaculate, picture-perfect house on hold. Caring for
multiples, even calm, easygoing ones, is a tremendous time commitment. Nothing can take the place of time spent with children. Take
shortcuts in other aspects of life, not with babies.

Laundry

The following ideas may simplify this task:

- If you wash diapers, do not fold them. Divide them into baskets
  directly from the dryer and use them from there. Disposable diapers or a diaper service saves even more time.
- You can throw the babies' laundry (except diapers) in with the
  family's wash unless any of the babies has sensitive skin.
- Forget owning an iron. Wear only wash and wear clothes that do
  not wrinkle when folded or hung immediately from the dryer.
- Let each family member put his or her clean clothes away.
  Preschoolers can do this if clothes are placed in small baskets.

- Place flannelette pads under each baby's head and/or diaper area in their cribs to avoid always changing an entire sheet.

Household Routine

The following suggestions may also help you streamline:

- Get some household help. A husband may offer his services, or hire someone part-time or full-time. (See Key 30.)
- Keep some infant clothing and diaper-changing paraphernalia, including diaper pails, on each level of your house.
- Bathe your babies every other day or less frequently. Keeping their diaper areas and faces clean is usually enough.
- Remove knickknacks now. That way there is less dusting and one less childproofing step to worry about later.
- Place a box or basket in each room to *toss* toys into and any room can be neat with minimal effort. Even toddlers can help.
- Use a Crock-pot and microwave oven to prepare meals conveniently.
- Use dried, frozen, and already chopped ingredients. Grocery store salad bars provide already chopped ingredients for casseroles as well as prewashed salad greens.
- Double recipes and freeze one meal to be used later.
- When ordering carryout, make use of healthy soup and salad bars instead of high-fat fast-food restaurants.
- Shop online or by catalog. You may pay a little more for some items, but save on others because you avoid impulse buying. Shopping online or using a 24-hour call center allows you to shop at odd times—such as after the 2 A.M. feedings.
- Consider using delivery services available in your area. Some grocery stores deliver or allow you to order online. There are milkmen in some areas, and they may carry other dairy products. A pharmacy that delivers prescriptions can deliver other items also.
- Become acquainted with all the drive-through services, such as dry cleaner, bank, photo finishing, and food.
- Make use of nonessential but helpful equipment, such as an answering machine, portable phone, and a food processor.
- Use the Internet to keep up with family and other parents.
- *Accept all offers of help.* Friends or relatives can go grocery shopping, bring a meal, fold laundry, vacuum, or wash dishes. When they ask what they can do to help, be specific.

33

COPING WITH CRYING

Crying is an important form of infant communication, but translating the cries of two or more babies can be overwhelming. A parent may feel there isn't enough of her/him to go around when more than one cries at once. When babies take turns, it can seem that every moment of the day is filled with their cries. When one baby cries more than the other(s), all babies still must be cared for and some parents feel guilty when one multiple receives more time and attention because of his crying.

Why Babies Cry

Newborns have only one form of verbal communication—crying, and nature designed babies' cries to get parents' attention. Crying may signal hunger, fatigue, overstimulation, discomfort, or some other form of distress. For some babies, crying is associated with temperament and an increased sensitivity. Some people believe that babies cry when parents feel tense, but the more likely scenario is that the babies' crying creates tension in their parents!

Most babies have very distinct cries for specific problems. The hunger cry is different from the "irritated because I'm wet" cry, which is different from the "I'm overtired" or "in pain" cries. Some cries and babies are easier to "read" than others. The cry of a chronically fretful, *high-need* baby may be tough to translate.

Babies cannot easily communicate discomfort or pain. An underlying health issue may be the source of crying, but the source of the problem is not always obvious. It is never easy to deal with a baby that is frequently uncomfortable, but it is even more difficult when no one can figure out the cause of a baby's discomfort. Parents and pediatric care providers should thoroughly investigate for possible physical causes of persistent crying.

Environmental substances appear to contribute to crying and fussiness in some babies. Any multiple might be sensitive to an ingredient in infant formula, such as the protein base (dairy or soy). A baby might be bothered by a substance that passes from mother's system into breast milk, although this is less likely unless there is a strong history of allergy on either side of the family. Certain babies may be bothered by supplementary vitamins or iron drops. (Discuss the situation with the pediatric care provider before changing any baby's diet.) Other irritants may include secondhand smoke, household sprays or powders, and additives in laundry products.

Handling the Trying Crying Times

There are many ways to cope with symphonic crying. Different coping techniques may work for different multiples or parents!

- Positive reminders of one's good fortune in having multiples can help. When out strolling with babies, enjoy all the compliments received from total strangers for the amazing feat of giving birth to and caring for multiples. Relish the praise heaped upon those adorable babies, even on days when it's difficult to believe.

- When fussiness or colic occurs at predictable times daily, invite helpers to provide the extra arms needed to comfort babies.

- Use infant equipment designed to soothe babies. Infant swings mechanically rock a baby and a baby's own motion rocks a bouncer seat. Go out for a walk and let the motion of the stroller and the fresh air soothe babies.

- Handling overstimulated babies may increase the level and duration of crying. If overstimulation is thought to be the problem after other possibilities have been ruled out, lay the crying baby in her crib in a quiet room to see if she settles down within five to ten minutes. Crying should decrease in intensity during that period, so try another intervention if intensity increases or baby continues to cry after ten minutes. *Do not let a baby continue to cry unattended.*

- "White noise," a rhythmic, staticky sound, such as that made by vacuum cleaner motor or a radio tuned to a spot between stations, is calming for some babies. Others are soothed by listening to the familiar sounds of the womb. Some infant equipment and electronic equipment shops sell devices that produce quiet white noises or tapes and CDs of uterine sounds.

Fretful, high-need babies often respond best to body contact:

- Find a comfortable rocking chair that fits one parent and at least two babies. Rocking with babies can calm everyone—a tense parent and the babies! Keep a folding lawn-chair rocker in the car for visits to rockerless relatives or friends.
- Soft infant carriers or slings allow a parent to keep babies close, yet one or both hands remain free. (See Appendix B: Resources—Slings/Carriers, for information or web sites.)
    - Double and triple infant-carriers are available.
    - Some parents use two single carriers together, "wearing" one baby in front and one in back, or crisscrossing both on the front of the body.
    - Two babies will fit in a single sling for some brands. Many parents crisscross two slings to wear a baby on each hip.
    - The ability to simultaneously carry two or three babies in carrier(s) or sling(s) depends on the "fit" between the parent's body and the babies' weights and activity levels.
    - Often only one baby "needs" to ride in a carrier or sling at any one time.
- It is never safe to walk while carrying more than one baby, since the adult would have no way to break a fall. However, many parents sometimes find each arm carrying a baby when walking. If this occurs, a parent must remain conscious of the dangers of carrying two until able to put one down. *Helpers should never be allowed to carry two babies at once.*

Cry Babies Are Good Babies

Parents are often asked if multiples are "good" babies, and most people assume "good" refers to the easily consoled, easygoing baby who is able to sleep for several hours—at night, of course—without interruption. This may leave a parent with the feeling that the fretful, high-need baby who wakes every one to three hours around the clock is "bad."

127

All babies are "good" babies, including the fretful, high-need kind. They may take more time and effort, and they may be more difficult to figure out when compared with a more easygoing member of the multiple set. However, it is not as if they cry and fret by choice. Their crying behavior is not a signal that these babies are manipulating their parents. Manipulation requires purposeful action, and babies are not capable of this. Signaling a need for food, comfort, and human contact is not manipulation.

A Parent's Feelings

It is common to feel ambivalent about multiples when one or more are particularly high-need babies. Obviously, baby care would be easier if all multiples were even-tempered rather than fretful, high-need, or colicky. Ambivalent feelings do not mean a parent would give any back if she/he could!

- Often sets of multiples include both easy-going and high-need babies. When two or more are high need, one usually is higher need than the other(s). Parents often feel torn when one requires more time and attention. However, they shouldn't feel concerned about responding to babies' individual needs.

  The more quiet one(s) usually "ask" for attention when it is needed. When time becomes available, spend some time alone with the "easier" one(s) to avoid the potential for benign neglect.
- It is natural to feel resentful at times when two or more babies are high-need or often difficult to comfort. That's okay. Face it, life *would* be more pleasant without all the crying.
- Negative feelings may be natural, but parents shouldn't take it out on the babies. Crying babies feel as frustrated as their parents. They would tell parents what they need if they could.
- Exercise, meditate, or scream into a pillow to release the pent-up frustration of coping with crying multiples. Cry along with the babies—it's as great a tension reliever for the parent as for the babies!
- Although resentful of a more fretful or high-need baby initially, a parent often feels closer sooner to the fussier baby, probably because the parent must interact more often with that baby.

34

~~~~~~

SLEEP

Sleep is a major concern for new parents of multiples. Strategies that work for a family with one infant are often inappropriate for families with multiples. Some babies sleep through the night almost immediately but most do not. It helps to be prepared to cope with this aspect of parenting more than one baby.

Fatigue related to the effects of multiple pregnancy and birth has an impact on a new mother's need for sleep. If she had a cesarean delivery, she is recovering from major surgery as well as childbirth. A woman may be pushing her body beyond its limits if she does not rest.

Unfortunately, parents' sleep needs and their babies' needs rarely coincide. Newborns cannot sleep for long periods without being fed. Sleeping four to five hours is sleeping through the night for young babies but many do not sleep this long. Most premies *must* be awakened and fed more often than this.

Realistic Expectations
Be realistic in what to expect. Babies need time to adjust to their new environment before parents worry about their sleep patterns.

- Multiples seldom disturb each other when they share a crib, and many sleep better. This is one reason NICUs are instituting multiples' co-bedding.
- Keep a sleep chart for each baby to help recognize individual patterns and see if the babies are each getting a typical amount of sleep.

Try

A parent's ability to manipulate their multiples' sleep-wake cycles depends on each baby's temperament and inherent body rhythms. One baby may be able to go along with whatever changes parents make, but another may resist every attempt to replace the natural cycle with an artificial routine. When attempting to modify the babies' routine, give anything tried a chance to work. It may take several days before any change is noticed.

Juggle sleeping arrangements until finding the one that works best for the entire family while still meeting the babies' needs. What works today may not work tomorrow. Be prepared to change, and be flexible.

If your babies are being bottlefed:

1. Alternate "night duty." One parent handles all infant care for all babies while the other parent sleeps through the night.
2. One of you can take the late evening feeding while the other goes to bed early and takes the middle of the night or early morning feedings. This usually gives each parent a four- to six-hour stretch of sleep.

If your babies are being fully breastfed:

1. A father cannot breastfeed babies, but he certainly can get out of bed, change the babies, bring them to mother to nurse, soothe a waiting baby, and then return them to their cribs.
2. Some fathers take over a night feeding by giving a bottle of expressed breast milk or formula to the babies so mother can get a few hours of uninterrupted sleep. This may be done only occasionally or every night. To avoid breast engorgement and related problems, it is best if a mother sleeps through only one feeding.
3. Another option used by some couples is for the mother to breastfeed one (or two) for all night feeds while her spouse bottle-feeds the other(s) at every feeding. Usually

parents alternate which babies are given the breast and which are given a bottle for every other feeding.

Distinguish nighttime from daytime. Keep the room dark and quiet at sleep times, and stimulate the babies as little as possible during feedings. Do not turn on the TV or radio to keep parents company.

Most parents prefer that their babies be on similar schedules. To accomplish this, try waking a second baby with or soon after the first awakens. Waking all higher-order multiples at once depends on the availability of extra hands to help with feedings.

The complaint of having "days and nights mixed up" is more intense for parents of multiples. Try waking them more frequently during the day to see if they lengthen their nighttime sleep periods.

Co-sleeping with Parents

The family bed has saved many a night's sleep for some parents. Parents who bring their twins to bed with them, even for part of the night, say the babies seem to wake less often and need less comforting. Co-sleeping with parents has been done for millennia and it still exists in most cultures, but safety has to be considered. Babies shouldn't sleep on waterbeds or be laid on "fluffy" pillows. Some experts recommend that only one baby at a time sleep with parents. There are also special baby beds that attach to the parents' bed. (See Appendix A for books on the family bed.)

Sleep Training

Proponents of sleep training methods do not suggest trying it until at least six to seven months for full-term babies. For preterm babies, count months from the due date, not the birth date.

The purpose of sleep training is to help older infants learn to self-soothe themselves to sleep. It does not mean letting any baby "cry it out." If they can go long periods without feeding, give them water instead of formula when they wake and/or rub their backs instead of picking them up. (See Appendix A for books on sleep training.)

Parents' Sleep

Each parent must evaluate his or her own sleep needs. You are not doing justice to yourself or your babies if you become a "walking zombie" because you are exhausted. Try to sleep when you sleep best, taking your own body rhythms into account.

• After the first hectic months, attempt to set a bedtime for the babies that allows you time to wind down before sleeping.
• Nap or rest during the day when the babies nap, if possible.
• Ask a friend or hire someone to babysit for a few hours while you sleep. Nap out of hearing range or have the care giver take your babies for a walk. You may not sleep if you hear them fussing.
• You might occasionally ask someone to spend the night and cover night feedings, especially with higher-order multiples or if one or more have ongoing health issues.
• Review the babies' sleep charts. You may discover a pattern that enables you to reorganize the routine to get more sleep.
• If you are a morning person, go to bed an hour earlier than usual at night.
• If you are a night person, occasionally arrange for someone else to get up with babies in the morning. Weekends provide the perfect opportunity for Dad to enjoy his babies while Mom sleeps in a little longer.

Night waking does not bother the babies; it bothers their parents. Infants who don't sleep through the night or have difficulty adjusting to change are not trying to be manipulative or thwart their parents. They simply are listening to their bodies just as parents want to listen to their bodies. As adults, both parents must readjust until each family member's sleep cycle is in sync with the others.

35

GETTING OUT

B oth parents and children benefit from the stimulation of a different environment than home on a regular basis. A long walk provides exercise for Mom and fresh air for babies or toddlers, which often improves everyone's mood and helps everyone sleep. Visits to friends or relatives often leave parents and multiples feeling refreshed and renewed. A trip to the shopping mall or to a fast food restaurant for lunch provides an adult environment and frequently some adult conversation even if venturing out alone with your multiples. Most parents of multiples are stopped repeatedly by curious strangers who ask questions and usually make positive comments when they see two, three, or more in a stroller.

Getting out with multiple infants or children requires organization, but with planning it can be accomplished. The effort involved will seem minimal once a system is developed, and it is worth every minute of organization to discover it is possible to get up and go with more than one!

Odds and Ends

Ask your multiples' pediatric care provider if it is safe to take them out where they will be in contact with others, especially if they were preterm, it is RSV season, one or more has an ongoing health issue, and so on. On the other hand, make yourself take them out once they've been given the "go ahead" by the care provider. Usually the benefits of outings outweigh the risks. If necessary, ask the care provider to help you face the fear that can result in overprotecting your babies from an exciting world.

You may enjoy the company and extra arms of a helper, especially if you have specific tasks to accomplish or you are heading out with higher-order multiples. However, don't be afraid to go out alone with multiples when no one is available to go with you even if you and they stroll no farther than the end of the street.

The Diaper or Babies' Bag

A well-stocked diaper bag contains a portable changing pad, a few more diapers than you think you'll need, extra clothing, a container of moistened wipes to clean messy hands or diaper areas, a stain remover stick for soiled clothing, and plenty of plastic bags for dirty diapers or soiled clothing. If you use bottles or pacifiers, bring a replacement or two in case any baby loses one or they fall or are dropped in an area where cleaning facilities aren't available. Have extra expressed breast milk or formula available in case you are gone from home longer than expected.

A small insulated bag and a freezer pack can be thrown in for items that require refrigeration, such as expressed breast milk, some forms of formula or solid foods, certain medications, etc. If any baby or toddler requires special equipment or medications for an ongoing health problem, find a bag with divided compartments to keep these items separate and easier to find.

Most parents of multiples prefer fairly large diaper bags. A roomy backpack is ideal. When worn correctly, the weight of the items inside is balanced, it can't fall forward into a baby if the parent changes position, and the parent has two arms free for babies. Other parents find a bag that can be slung over the shoulder works best. Some bags can be attached to the frames of certain strollers. If looking at a bag and stroller arrangement, be certain that the weight of the bag won't tip the stroller and any babies in it if one or more babies is removed. Also, make certain that the attached diaper bag will be out of babies' reach. Some parents find it is easier to carry and maintain two smaller diaper bags. A parent may carry one and attach the other to the stroller.

Many mothers place purses, or the essential items they usually carry, into a diaper bag compartment so they have one less item to juggle. If you do this, be sure it isn't accessible to others when you are preoccupied with babies. A fanny pack is another alternative to free hands yet safeguard important items.

Restock the diaper bag with essential items as soon as you return home from any outing or before you go to bed each night. This routine will save time if you are ever in a rush trying to get everyone ready to go somewhere, yet it frees you from the worry that you might have left home without some critical baby care item.

Car Seats

The use of an approved car seat for each baby or toddler is the law in the United States. In many states a baby cannot be discharged from the hospital without proof that the parents have a car seat for the baby to make the trip home and for use during every car ride thereafter. *Always* buckle each child into an approved car seat, whether traveling for ten seconds or ten hours. (See Key 10 for information about purchasing car seats.)

Many car seats also may be used as infant carriers; however, carrying even one baby by the handle of a car seat can be awkward and cause muscle strain for a parent. Carrying two babies at once may cause additional strain. Also, some pediatric care providers have expressed concern that a baby could fall if the plastic handle breaks or if the handle slips or is bumped. It may be better for parents to move each baby to the stroller or cart seat or place one or more in a sling or cloth carrier worn on the parent's body.

The Stroller

A stroller designed for multiples may be *the* essential piece of equipment when on foot. It truly can be a lifeline to the outside world. It empowers and allows a parent to feel more in control by providing the means and the flexibility to leave home with two or more babies or toddlers without the help of another adult.

These suggestions may help streamline outings:

- Store the stroller in your car or place it there the night before an anticipated outing. Then you will have one less trip to the car when getting everyone ready to leave the house.
- Don't leave home without the stroller even if you don't plan to use it during an outing. A multiple stroller provides multiple infant seats or multiple high chairs for use in others' homes.

135

Also, if you would ever have car trouble you may need to remove all the babies from the car, which would be difficult to manage without the stroller.

- If you want to increase skin contact with your babies or you do not want to attract attention while out, place one (or more) in a baby sling or a carrier and place any other(s) in a stroller. By the time most people realize how many babies you have with you, you will have passed them. People also are less likely to stop you if you avoid making eye contact with them. (For information about purchasing or using slings or soft carriers with two or more babies at once, see Appendix B: Resources.)

- If any toddler multiples are climbers, secure them in a stroller seat by using harnesses that attach to the stroller frame. Also, zip-up-the-back harnesses usually work best because they are less accessible to clever little fingers.

At the Market

Every family needs food, so the grocery store is often the first place a parent of multiples ventures with babies. You may want to develop some shopping guidelines, because distractions can easily result in inattention to babies. Although the ideas refer to multiples, the ideas for use with higher-order multiples may be adapted if you are taking twins and an older child shopping.

For all multiples. Many markets have shopping carts with built-in infant seats. If these are not available, some infant or car seats fit snugly into the seat portion of a large cart. Bring the cart(s) to your car rather than take the babies in their seats to the cart(s).

Any infant seat placed within a cart seat should be buckled into the seat portion of the cart. (Baby should be buckled into the infant seat, plus the infant seat should be strapped into the cart.) Do not leave an infant seat within the cart seat area if unable to get a snug fit or buckle the infant seat to the cart seat area. A baby can fall from a wobbling or unsecured seat.

One cart/twins. Place one baby in an infant seat secured to the seat portion of the cart. Wear the second baby in a sling or infant carrier. Store items are then placed in the basket of the cart. (Some mothers wear two in a sling or carrier, but you need to be able to do so and still have a free hand for shopping.)

An alternative method is to place a second infant seat (and baby) in the basket portion of the cart when one baby/infant seat already is riding in the cart seat. It is dangerous to pile items around a baby in a seat in the basket area, so groceries can be placed in a second cart that you pull behind. Babies should be pushed in the front cart so you can keep an eye on and interact with them.

One or two carts/higher-order multiples. Most parents of higher-order multiples take a mother's helper or two when they go to the grocery store or they leave one or two babies at home. However, it may be possible to go alone with babies if you go during a calm time of the day for most or all of them.

For three babies, secure one in an infant seat in the cart seat, the second in an infant seat placed in the basket area, and wear the third in a sling or carrier. Pull a second cart for the groceries. (Read the directions above for twins.)

If you don't want to use a sling or carrier or you are shopping with quads, a third baby could ride in an infant seat secured in the cart seat area of the second cart. Grocery items would be placed in the basket area of the pulled cart.

Older babies and toddler multiples. When babies are able to sit well, use seatbelts or harnesses to hold each securely in a separate cart seat. Some markets have carts with two seats on one cart for carrying older babies or toddlers. A third child could ride in a baby backpack or sling if a parent wanted to use only one cart. If using two carts, divide market items between carts.

Staying safe when shopping. Remain alert and cautious whenever you use a shopping cart. Babies can fall out of improperly secured infant seats. A baby in an infant seat that is placed in the cart's basket area can be injured if the seat tips within the cart or if items fall on a baby because a parent piled them around the seat.

Older babies enjoy reaching for things on shelves, which can be a problem if a fallen item hits a baby or the floor!

If any multiples are climbers, secure them in a cart seat by using zip-up-the-back harnesses attached to the cart frame. Many toddlers escape from the seatbelts provided with cart seats.

Once multiples sit well, it is *never* safe to seat any in the basket of the cart without a seatbelt or harness. A child may stand to reach something interesting on a shelf and fall out when a parent is preoccupied. Falls from carts are associated with numerous injuries and hospital emergency room visits every year. Carts are designed to hold unmoving objects only. A cart can overturn by a shift in movement of even one young child.

Two or more children in the basket of a cart are an accident waiting to happen. Not only do they often encourage each other to grab items on shelves, which can lead to falls, they also are more likely to rush to one end causing the cart to overturn.

Taking Only One

When someone can help care for multiples at home, consider taking only one baby or toddler on an outing. This can be a treat for a parent and each child. For instance, one mother alternated taking one baby to church because it gave her and each baby an hour alone. Another took one baby when she went to the grocery store. These mothers enjoyed the opportunity to focus calmly on one multiple, and each multiple enjoyed mother's undivided attention. It can help to plan one-to-one excursions for calm periods or the naptime of the one(s) left home, so any baby left at home is less likely to become upset.

Human beings generally crave socialization and mobility. It may be more of a challenge to venture forth with multiples, but the psychological and emotional rewards for both parents and children make the effort worthwhile.

36

~~~~~~

GROWTH AND DEVELOPMENT

THREE TO SIX MONTHS

The second three months of infants' lives are characterized by a growing awareness of the environment and the special persons caring for them. Most parents are aware by the third month that life is settling into a "new normal" routine even when it's not quite there yet. However, parents may be so busy caring for multiple babies and racing through household chores that they don't have time to stop and recognize that a daily pattern of life is emerging or that they have become masters of organization and efficiency.

Life with Multiples

Babies become increasingly social between three to six months. Each eagerly interacts with parents and others in the environment. Each begins to recognize as special the person, usually Mother in Western cultures, who cares for him or her the most.

- There is nothing to compare with the importance of being the center of the universe for multiple babies. Could there be a better reward for all the time and attention you spend with each than to see their faces light up simultaneously and their numerous arms and legs begin to wave wildly when you enter the room?
- Babies usually do not interact much with each other at this age, although one multiple may initiate physical contact with another, such as touching another's hand or arm when they are laid side by side. Two babies may sometimes make eye contact. In addi-

tion, they may end up on top of each other when placed in the same crib. However, each probably will be more fascinated with getting to know his or her own hands and feet than the other multiple(s) during these months.

- Smiling is an important form of interaction by three months, but not every baby is as lavish with smiles as another. Although all should smile spontaneously at times, don't expect an equal number of smiles from each multiple. Don't take it personally if any baby's temperament makes him or her seem stingy with smiles. Also, do not equate a baby's more sober look as unhappiness. Some babies simply seem to be more serious by nature. Do make the pediatric care provider aware, however, if any baby rarely or never smiles.

- Most parents feel more in tune with each baby's behavioral style during the second three months, and trial and error has taught them which soothing techniques work best with each baby. However, the subtleties of each baby's personality may still seem elusive as differentiation continues. (See Key 23.)

- Colic usually disappears and fussy spells tend to diminish during these months. Most babies are easier to comfort by now. However, irritable behavior is not unusual at times, especially when any of the babies is overtired or hungry, or needs some human contact.

- A "high need," or supersensitive, multiple will continue to require more from parents, and parents should continue to respond to the cues of each baby. It isn't possible to treat multiples equally. It also isn't necessary to treat all in the same way, since each is an individual with a different need for time and attention.

- (If multiples had to spend several weeks in a NICU after birth as a result of prematurity or illness, there may be a delay in the three to sixth month timeline.) Still multiples that were preterm, growth-restricted, or sick at birth usually look and act more like "regular" babies when they reach three to six months. Most parents feel more comfortable handling them by this time, too. However, some parents have trouble believing their babies are now healthy. These parents may overprotect their "fragile" babies, or they may have difficulty forming an attachment with one or more who were sick. If the babies have been given a clean bill of health, yet you continue to see them as fragile, discuss your feelings with the pediatric care provider.

Growth and Development

Research indicates that multiple-birth infants receive less physical and verbal stimulation from parents than single-born infants. Immersed in infant care tasks, some parents apparently talk to and play with multiples less. Yet each multiple needs the kind and amount of stimulation as any single infant to promote physical and verbal skill development.

Providing the stimulation that encourages optimal development for each multiple does not take much additional time because it can be incorporated into infant care tasks. However, each parent must make a point to take advantage of opportunities to provide stimulation while getting another job done. To encourage optimal development of each multiple:

- Recognize that you are the most interesting toy any of your babies will ever have.
  - Seize any moment available to establish eye contact and interact with one alone, whether changing that baby's diaper, wiping a face, or simply sharing a quiet moment. Those minutes add up.
  - If a physical or occupational therapist is working with any multiple, ask the therapist to show you how to repeat the exercises. Practice with the baby while accomplishing other care-giving tasks. (Many of these exercises are appropriate and fun for all the babies.)
  - Do not lose any opportunity to give one a hug or a kiss or to reinforce a baby's name. A baby can be hugged, kissed, and told, "I love you, (insert name)" all at the same time. Individual infant massage provides a wonderful way to connect with each baby.
  - Alternate making eye contact and playing with one baby. This may be done when holding more than one, or a parent

141

can kneel at the babies' feet as they lay next to one another on a pad or blanket on the floor. (This is a great method for diaper changing assembly-line style.) No matter how many babies a parent may be touching, it is possible to look in the eyes of only one baby at once.

– As you make eye contact and play with one multiple, call that baby by name. Each needs to hear that name during any period of eye contact in order to eventually understand that a certain name "belongs" only to him or her. Sometimes show each baby his or her reflection in a mirror as you call the baby by name. Also, your multiples may be babies, but they already are beginning to learn how they are valued as an individual and as part of a set.

– Mimic the face and sounds each baby makes. Make eye contact with that baby to let her or him know a repeat performance is desired. Don't be afraid to create faces or sounds so babies can mimic you.

– Talk to each baby as you care for him or her. Describe and explain what they are seeing in their home as you carry each from room to room, or as you push them in their stroller outside. Ask each of them questions. Although they are too young to respond, each is learning how expression changes language.

– Remember that a parent's arms remain the superior infant carrier even if you sometimes need the help of extra "arms" in the form of bouncer chairs or wind-up swings. The stimulation each baby receives when carried in your arms or sitting in your lap cannot be replaced by any piece of equipment.

• Be alert for, applaud and encourage each baby's efforts to reach every new milestone, whether it is one's interest in a rattle or another's attempts to roll over.

• Look in specialty catalogs for age-appropriate developmental toys. The sizes, colors, and textures designed for toys for this age group usually promote some aspect of infant development. Often a parent can take the concepts incorporated in these developmental toys and substitute an item found in the home.

- Monitor each baby's progress for three to six month olds as described in a respected book about infant growth and development. Pay attention to discussion on normal variations for the age group, especially for fraternal multiples, who are likely to reach developmental milestones at different times. Consult the babies' pediatric care provider if you have questions or ever feel concerned about any baby's development.

    – If multiples were premature, especially if they were extremely premature, standard infant growth and development timetables probably will have to be adjusted for multiples' expected (full-term) "due date" rather than actual (preterm) birth date. Ask their pediatric care provider when they might be expected to "catch up" with children sharing their actual birth date.

    – Prematurity, low birth weight, and significant illness at birth can be associated with developmental delays that are unrelated to expected due date versus actual birth date. Therefore, these multiples should be routinely screened for delays during the first several years. Early diagnosis of a delay and immediate intervention can have a tremendous impact on a child's development. It is important to balance realistic expectations for babies who may need time to catch up with legitimate concerns that any is lagging behind in development. If ever feeling concerned about any baby, be sure to bring the concern to the attention of the pediatric care provider with a reminder about that baby's history.

Daily Routine

Most babies have established a fairly predictable daily routine by three months. However, the routine that develops for any given multiple is not necessarily what a parent considers ideal!

- Babies generally are awake for longer periods by three months and many babies begin to sleep for at least one longer stretch of time.

- Parents usually can predict the approximate times that each baby will nap, sleep at night, and wake for night feedings by three to six months. Although a multiple might be ready to sleep longer periods at night, the need of the other(s) for night feedings often continues. Babies are developing a sense of trust in themselves and finding out they can depend on parents during their first year, so it is extremely important that they be responded to and have their needs met when they indicate the need for human contact—night and day. (See Key 34.)
- Identical twins are more likely to demonstrate similar wake and sleep patterns. Their naps tend to occur in the same number and at the same times without any encouragement from parents. The number of naps and the timing of sleep for fraternal multiples can be quite different. Some fraternal multiples are able to adapt more easily than others if parents encourage more similar sleep patterns.
- When healthy multiples have different body clocks, some parents have success waking one multiple to feed with or immediately after another during their second three months even if they had no luck trying it the first three months. However, the opposite also has occurred. A multiple that willingly woke and fed with or immediately after another during the first three months, sometimes resists or becomes upset if awakened when older.
- If you have been waking one baby with or immediately after another for night feedings, it may be time to see what happens if you let that second baby sleep. It is possible to miss a baby's readiness to sleep for a longer stretch, or through the night, when continuing to wake a sleeping baby.

Factors affecting routine. The development of a household routine may be common by three to six months, but there are factors that may affect its emergence.

- It may take more time for a routine to evolve if multiples' behavioral responses vary widely, any multiple is a high-need baby, or any two multiples frequently flip-flop temperament traits whenever a parent thinks she is finally able to predict how each baby will respond to a given situation.

144

- When multiples were premature and spent weeks in an NICU before arriving home, a daily routine may develop from the NICU routine. Many preterm multiples seem happy to stick with the feeding and sleep schedule they became accustomed to in the NICU. However, other babies seem to want to make up for lost time by requiring around-the-clock time and attention once they realize they are in a different environment. Of course, it is common to have a baby who continues with the NICU timetable and another who requires a more flexible routine.

- The development of a routine may take more time if any baby is affected by certain ongoing health problems that require special care at home. Still, most parents report they feel familiar with and have a routine for health-care procedures and using related equipment by three to six months, unless a baby's health status suddenly changes and requires a change in procedure or equipment use.

Feedings

Most babies have established feeding routines by the time they reach three months. There are a few changes in feeding, however, that may occur during the three to six month period.

- Babies interact more with the person feeding them between three to six months. Continue to hold each for feedings. Both you and they benefit from the increased social contact at their mealtimes.

- Most breastfed babies experience another so-called "growth spurt" at some time between 12 and 15 weeks and again at about six months. Growth spurts are associated with more frequent feedings for two or three days. If multiples show signs of a growth spurt at the same time, the increased feedings may last for four to six days. Multiples also may experience growth spurts one after another, so that it may take one or two weeks for all babies to go through it.

- Multiples may drop a feeding or two between three to six months whether breast- or bottle-fed. With luck all will drop a night feeding! (Some breastfed babies drop a feeding soon after requesting more frequent feedings during a several-day growth spurt.)

- Multiples that still prefer more frequent feedings usually become extremely efficient at feeding during the second three months, so feedings take much less time. They may empty a breast or bottle and feel satisfied within minutes. When an older baby begins to breastfeed in less than five minutes, mothers sometimes are concerned the baby isn't getting enough to eat. They may not recognize that the baby simply has become more efficient, especially if other multiples enjoy longer nursing sessions. By counting a baby's wet and dirty diapers, a mother can compare it with the typical count for this baby. Unless either number decreases significantly, the change in feeding pattern would be considered as normal.

- Babies become easily distracted during feedings toward the end of the second three months. If any sees or hears something nearby, the baby will likely stop feeding to check it out. This may include another multiple feeding simultaneously.

- Occasionally a baby indicates readiness for solid food before six months. Early readiness is the exception, however, not the rule. Never feed anything to babies other than breast milk or infant formula before first discussing it with the babies' pediatric care provider. There are reasons to wait to introduce solid foods, and certain foods are more appropriate to offer first. (To coordinate spoon feedings, see Key 37.)

Three to six months often is a period of relative calm after the wild storm of the first few months period of adjustment. Enjoy and appreciate it. Look back and see how far you and your family have come. Be sure to give yourself a well-deserved pat on the back!

37

GROWTH AND DEVELOPMENT

SIX TO NINE MONTHS

Six to nine months is a period of transition for babies. For most, a once all-liquid diet now begins to include solid foods. Many babies move from parents' laps to the floor as their mobility increases and they begin to explore the frontiers of home. Keeping up with the challenges of supervising two or more babies who are learning to go on their own can be exciting.

Growth and Development

Motor development. Differences related to "twin type" often become more obvious as multiples evolve into older babies. Each one's appearance, behavioral style, and activity level becomes more sharply defined as they accelerate in their achievement of developmental milestones.

Fraternal multiples' approaches to developmental skills often vary, particularly for multiples of opposite sex. One baby may focus more on gaining large motor ability while another concentrates on developing fine motor control. Often each baby has a completely different approach for developing the same skill.

Identical multiples frequently work on developing the same skills at the same time. They tend to go about learning a new skill in exactly the same way even when neither can observe the other.

New frontiers. You, and everything in your home, are your babies' most important developmental toys. They learn every minute by touching and tasting, observing and listening. Now when holding any baby, a parent can expect to be poked and prodded as

147

each learns about noses, mouths, ears, hair, and any items in the vicinity of the parent's face, such as earrings, barrettes, or hats.

Every object they encounter has color and sound, texture and form—the fabrics of various pieces of furniture, the metal and plastic kitchen utensils and eating ware, the change in floor coverings from room to room, the curves and angles of items that fit in their hands. Each baby registers all these experiences in the brain and organizes this information for future use.

Whether any multiple is a more "physical" learner while another seems to learn more by being an "observer," all babies of this age are compelled to physically experience objects with their hands and by then putting them in their mouths.

Parents of multiples may find the intermittent use of equipment, such as play yards or saucer seats necessary for survival. However, it is important to avoid the overuse or abuse of such equipment. The temptation to place babies in such equipment may be greater when keeping track of mobile multiples, but for optimal development of babies' bodies and brains, they depend on opportunities to explore their home while crawling and cruising about on their own arms and legs.

Childproofing becomes crucial once any baby begins to roll or scoot; it can save parents' sanity and many breakable items. (Include each baby as a breakable item, too!) When babies travel in different directions at once, parents are able to relax if the environment has been made safe for their pint-sized pioneers. (See Key 39.)

Verbal skills. Babies begin to make sounds in a more purposeful way between six to nine months. Your multiples may work very hard to repeat the sounds they hear. Whenever possible:

- Establish eye contact with any baby making sounds and mimic the sounds the baby is making.
- Verbally identify the objects any baby is observing, touching, or tasting.
- Continue to describe and explain the environment of their home and neighborhood. Parents can never talk to any or all of their multiples too much.

• Continue to make opportunities to call each multiple by name. Each baby's fascination with her or his reflection in a mirror only continues to grow at this age, so take advantage of mirror play to point to a baby and then to the baby's reflection while reinforcing the baby's name. A single-born infant recognizes his or her name when called by nine months. It is a reasonable goal that each multiple-birth infant should be able to do the same.

Other developments. Most babies begin *teething* and experience the eruption of several front teeth between six and nine months. However, teeth sometimes don't "pop" through until after a baby's first birthday. Some babies are irritable when teething, and others never seem bothered. Often every new tooth of identical multiples appears in the mouth of each within days, and sometimes hours, of the other. Yet one fraternal multiple can have several teeth, and have them for months, before another has any.

Babies tend to catch more *minor illnesses* at six to nine months. Whatever one contracts, the other(s) are likely to catch also. The first baby with a contagious disease exposes the other(s) to it before the first displays any symptoms. It usually is impossible to prevent this, although special precautions may be worth the effort if one baby already has a compromising health condition.

Parents should continue to chart *preterm* multiples' development more according to due date than by actual birth date, especially if multiples were very preterm, or less than 33 weeks gestation at birth.

Multiples who once were happy to go to any pair of extra arms may become picky and want only a parent or someone who is with them almost every day by the end of the eighth month. It is about this time that most babies develop some degree of *stranger anxiety*. One baby may be affected more than the other(s).

Solid Foods

Introducing solid foods may be an exciting step in multiples' development, but it is not a step to hurry. Although others may encourage you to offer solids by suggesting it will help babies sleep longer or act more content, research does not support this. Readiness for a new food experience should guide the introduction of solid foods, and multiples may be ready at different times.

Before introducing solid food to any baby, discuss the "when" and the "how to" of each new kind of food with the babies' pediatric care provider. Introducing solids before a baby is physically ready to swallow from a spoon can be an exercise in futility, as their tongues push the food back out as quickly as an adult spoons it in. Introducing solids before a baby's system is mature enough to digest them may provide bulk but it has no nutritional value. It also may introduce a sensitive baby to a potential allergen.

Few babies possess the ability to swallow solid foods easily or digest them well before four months. (Based on age if full term at birth.) Most babies are ready to try solid food at six or seven months. However, some babies may not need or show interest in solid foods until eight or nine months.

In addition to reaching the middle of the first year, other signs that a baby may be ready for solid foods include the baby's ability to hold its head up when in a sitting position, acting interested or reaching for food when others are eating, and anticipating a bite to eat by opening the mouth when offered food. Also, a breastfed baby may seem to be in the midst of a growth spurt that continues well beyond a few days.

Don't introduce solids to all babies at once simply because they are multiples. Each baby should let you know when she or he is ready for this new food experience, regardless of the other(s). Don't be surprised if each signals readiness in a different way. When feeding solid foods to multiples, other information may be helpful.

- Identical multiples tend to be ready and interested in starting solids at about the same time. Fraternal multiples' readiness or interest can vary by weeks or months.
- Because *preterm* babies' systems may need more time to mature, they may be older before any of them are ready to handle solid

foods. Discuss the benefits and risks of offering solid foods to "former" premies with their pediatric care provider.

- Although the iron in breast milk is better digested and many formulas contain iron, some preterm multiples or an identical multiple that was the "donor" in twin-to-twin transfusion syndrome (TTTS) may need supplementary iron drops. The pediatric care provider can determine if additional iron is needed by running a simple blood test available in many pediatric offices.
- Breastfeed *before* offering solid food in order to maintain milk production. Also, mothers may want to delay introducing other liquids, such as infant juices, to breastfed multiples.
- When spoon-feeding multiples simultaneously, place them side-by-side in infant seats, high chairs, or stroller. Use one bowl and one spoon. Alternate bites with babies.
- Each baby may wait more patiently for a bite of solid food if given a spoon or a small toy to hold while they are being fed.
- When both parents are available for a meal, each should be responsible for feeding babies. Divide babies between parents, alternating which parent feeds which baby so everyone gets some individual time together.
- It may save time and trouble to feed babies their solid food meal before the rest of the family sits down, but babies can be part of a family gathering when they sit in high chairs at the table while the rest of the family eats. Younger babies can be given small toys to play with and older babies may enjoy experimenting with a new finger food as they enjoy time with the family.
- Babies still need the security of being held in a parent's arms for some feedings. Older babies often pat a mother's breasts, want to hold their own bottles, or hold each other's hand while they are being held during a feeding.
- Many parents want to make some or all of their babies' solid foods rather than purchase commercial baby foods. Some want to save money; others prefer that their babies eat "natural" foods. Many adult foods are appropriate for infants if cooked and pureed appropriately and spices are not added. However, a few table foods should not be offered during babies' first year, so learn the principles of making baby food first.

- Switching from infant formula to cow's milk may seem a good way to cut costs when there are multiples to feed, but the American Academy of Pediatrics discourages this. They recommend that all babies continue to be breastfed or remain on infant formula for at least their first 12 months, and this period may need to be extended for multiples that were preterm at birth or those having certain health conditions.

Routine

A daily routine continues to evolve as multiples spend more time occupied with motor skill development. The development of babies' motor skills may interfere with a routine that had been operating for weeks or months. Parents often adapt to the changes in a single baby with little effort. However, a change in the behavior or abilities of one baby affects all in a set of multiples and parents are more aware of the disruption to routine.

- One or all multiples may drop a nap between six to nine months. Often a morning nap is the one to go.
- One or all may lengthen the time between breast- or bottle-feedings as their interest in solid food increases.
- More frequent baths may become a necessity as babies spend more time on the floor or discover and share creative uses for solid food. Most multiples enjoy bathing with one another once they are able to sit unsupported. Bathing babies together also saves parents' time and energy. (But see Key 39.)
- It is not unusual for any baby to begin waking again, or more often, at night during this period. Whether due to teething, an increase in minor illnesses, the onset of stranger anxiety, or some other reason, it often is difficult to ascertain.

Six to nine months is an exciting period in multiples' development. As the babies become more preoccupied with the environment, you will have more time to appreciate the differences and similarities of their individual styles. You also may find you have a little more time for yourself and other family members.

38

~~~~~~

GROWTH AND DEVELOPMENT

9 TO 15 MONTHS

Babies enter this stage on all fours but they walk or run through its exit! It may be a challenge to stay one step ahead of multiples at this age. When they give you a moment to slow down, you probably will be captivated by the blossoming relationship between or among them. This Key provides a glimpse of a fascinating period in multiples' development and a few suggestions for smoothing a parent's pathway through it. (Also see Key 39.)

Growth and Development

Physical and motor development. Multiples stay busy refining "old" skills and learning new ones during this stage. Each baby's personality truly unfolds, and all are likely to spend much more time physically and/or visually interacting with one another. "Twin type" differences often come more into focus.

Identical multiples usually have compensated for any great difference in physical traits that might have been present at birth. Typically, their growth patterns, weights, heights, hair growth pattern as well as its color and texture, and skin tones are very close by this time. Identical multiples still look different to their parents, but it's not unusual for parents to find themselves doing an occasional but momentary doubletake to identify one or the other.

As with other aspects of their behavioral styles, identical multiples tend to be closer in motor development and activity levels. Both or all usually lean toward being more "physical," or all are more of the "observer" type. All work hard at developing gross motor skills or all are more involved with fine motor control.

Fraternal multiples' motor development and/or activity levels may be similar or at opposite ends for normal deviation in development. Any male in a set with both genders is more likely to have a higher level of activity and be more gross motor-oriented.

Language development. Older babies and toddlers continue to make purposeful sounds, and they often attempt to say particular words. Parents can encourage speech development by repeating the sound or word any baby makes while making eye contact with that multiple and by pointing to the objects any multiple names.

Each multiple should recognize his or her name and image in a mirror by 15 months. If any baby does not respond to his or her name, make a game of pointing to a particular baby while saying that baby's name. Some multiples, especially identical multiples, become confused and look to the other multiple(s) when seeing a reflection in the mirror. If any frequently acts confused when seeing his or her reflection in a mirror, say the baby's name while pointing to his or her reflection in a mirror and then point to the baby while repeating the name.

The ability to use speech is called *expressive language*, and *receptive language* is the ability to understand it. Expect differences in multiples' abilities to actually say words or phrases, but there should be little difference in their understanding of language.

Each multiple should be able to understand several dozen words and be able to respond to simple requests by 15 months (based on full-term birth date). If any multiple has difficulty with receptive language at 15 to 16 months, it is important to bring this to the attention of the pediatric care provider.

There is tremendous variation in the development of expressive language. Girls tend to be verbal before their brothers, and one multiple may talk long before another. When there are differences in toddler multiples' verbal abilities, parents sometimes feel concerned unnecessarily.

Encourage a less verbal multiple to "speak" up rather than letting a more verbal one speak for him or her. This provides opportunities to practice words and also makes parents aware of any having difficulty with receptive language. Most toddlers can communicate their desires or opinions in some way if they understand what is being said.

Other developments. Separation anxiety is common for older babies and toddlers, and most let their parents know loudly and clearly that they prefer to be in their parents' care. However, many multiples are less affected by separation anxiety than a single child as long as two multiples can remain together. Parents are one "home base" in terms of feelings of security, but each multiple(s) may develop a second "home base" in the other(s).

A multiple might now resist going out alone with a parent because of their increasing involvement with the other multiple(s). One also might become angry if another multiple goes on a separate outing with a parent, because they are unable to understand the idea of taking turns at this age.

The realization that one has formed an individual relationship with each multiple may strike a parent during this period. This seems to occur earlier if parents have boy-girl twins and later if multiples are identical.

Feeding

Your multiples' diets begin to look more "grown up" during this period, as they move from pureed foods to more table and finger foods. Each may signal readiness for new foods and develop feeding skills at different times and in different ways.

- Self-feeding by each is easiest in the long run. Initially, you may have to combine spoon and self-feeding, but present each baby with a bowl containing a small amount of food and a spoon as soon as you notice any baby using the thumb and index finger (pincer grasp) to pick up things.

155

- Give them liquids in small cups with handles or a cup their hands can encircle. Nondrip sip cups that have lids with a spout were designed for babies this age (or a little younger). They are baby-manageable and less messy.
- Introduce finger foods as soon as possible at about nine months. It is easier to help one baby or take a bite of one's own meal if the other(s) are able to eat something without help from a parent.

The combination of two or more babies, high activity levels, and finger foods can result in "food fights." Remove each perpetrator's food and explain why. Return the food after a minute or two. Repeat this process if a food fight recurs. Moving high chairs farther apart often helps maintain order at mealtimes.

Toddler multiples seem to find some interesting uses for foods. It may help to think of this as a sign of creative development!

Between food fights and multiples' interesting uses for food, two or more babies will "lose" food to the floor. Place a drop cloth under high chairs for easier clean up.

Many multiples wean during this period, although it isn't unusual for them to continue breastfeeding or take a bottle. Identical multiples are more likely to wean at about the same time; fraternal multiples may be ready together or wean months apart. Also, one may seem ready to wean but continue to breastfeed or bottle-feed as long as the other(s) continues.

Physical growth and appetites normally slow by 12 to 15 months, but the nutritional needs of multiples may differ. Even identical multiples that are growing at the same rate may eat different amounts or kinds of foods. One may eat more at a particular meal and another may prefer a heavier meal at a different time of day.

First Birthday

Hooray! You made it! This birthday may be more of a celebration for their parents than for the one-year-old multiples, but they don't understand the significance of birthdays, anyway—at least not yet! Your multiples will not care whether the entire extended family and neighborhood is present or if you alone commemorate their special day with them. Party plans should coincide with your needs and the time you are willing to spend preparing for guests.

Their first birthday provides the perfect opportunity to reaffirm each baby's individuality although, as a set, they obviously share this special day. Remind guests who might bear gifts that separate persons comprise a set of multiples. They are not a collective entity.

Bake or buy (or beg from Grandma) small individual cakes or cupcakes, or divide a sheet cake into individual sections and decorate a section for each. Sing "Happy Birthday" to one and then another, taking turns until the song has been sung to each. (Some families alternate which multiple is sung to first, starting with the baby born first for this year, the baby born second for the second birthday, and so on.) Or sing only once, but refer to each baby by name rather than singing, "Happy birthday dear twins (triplets, quads, quints, and so on)."

Ready or Not!

Newly mobile multiples can be entertaining and exasperating whirlwinds of activity. Their newfound preoccupation with one another can have both pleasant and perilous consequences. Do not sit back and relax just yet; older toddler multiples are even busier and more interesting!

39

CHILDPROOFING THEIR WORLD

C reating a safe environment demands extra parental thought and action when multiples create distractions. Parents must be more aware of potential dangers. Parents of multiples must fine-tune their skills of observation and anticipation.

Every Age

Certain safety adages apply for multiples of all ages.

- Often one is injured when a parent is preoccupied with the other(s).
- Situations that are hazardous with one baby often are exaggerated for more than one.
- It is easy to underestimate each multiple's physical or mental capabilities when dealing with different developmental timetables.
- The more physically active each is, the more challenging and crucial childproofing becomes.
- Whether because of gender-related differences or socialization, boys are more likely to engage in risk-taking behaviors resulting in injuries.
- It may take twice as long to buckle and unbuckle, but *never* start the car until all children are properly restrained in car seats (or seat belts if older).

Most of the suggestions that follow should be multiplied as your babies grow!

Newborn to Six Months

Unsafe equipment, misuse of equipment, and falls are most often responsible for accidents during the first half year.

- Do not borrow or buy used equipment, such as cribs and car seats, unless *certain* that it meets safety guidelines.
- *Never* lay a baby on or in anything above floor level unless you are next to *and* paying attention to that baby or the side rails are locked in place. The baby lying quietly today may roll off the changing table or sofa tomorrow. The baby in an infant seat up on a table may bounce until the seat falls off or may pitch forward out of it.
- Lower crib mattresses once any baby begins to roll over.
- Get down on all fours and childproof your home for the next stage.

Six to Nine Months

Curiosity is crucial, but budding explorers require additional safeguarding.

Multiples *quickly* find any neglected hazard. Move breakable curios and all cleaning agents and plants beyond their reach. Cap electrical outlets and move electrical cords now. Scan the floor frequently for small, "edible" items.

Never leave any multiple unsupervised—even briefly—when their movements are confined by equipment, such as play yards or walkers. Walkers especially are associated with a large number of emergency room visits each year.

Never leave any child unattended in the tub. While distracted with one child or getting postbath clothing, another could turn on the hot water, slip and fall, or drown in as little as one inch of water.

Nine to Fifteen Months

New safety challenges arise as multiples begin to toddle on two feet and become more interested in each other. Together multiples can create more mischief than a single toddler.

- Use safety gates to keep multiples *in* or *out* of an area. Gate the top and bottom of stairways, but a couple of bottom steps could be left open so they can practice climbing.

- Keep the door to the cellar locked. Basement stairways are often open and uncarpeted, which make them even more dangerous.
- When multiples are in the kitchen, use safety latches on all drawers and cabinets except for one "play" drawer. *Never* leave any child in the kitchen without adult supervision. Use gates to keep them out when a parent is not there.
- Bathrooms should be off-limits. A toilet draws toddler multiples like a magnet. Not only do they put things into it, toddlers have drowned in toilets after falling forward head first.
- Use chest harnesses for climbers who want out of the stroller, high chairs, and shopping cart. It is more difficult to get out of a harness that fastens in the back, even with a sibling's help. Harnesses with side straps and a leash option are more adaptable.
- Hard-soled, heavy, high-top shoes are generally an unnecessary expense and they can become weapons when kicking or hitting at the others. Flexible, soft-soled gym shoes are safer, and they support and protect early walkers' feet just as well or better.

Special Hazards

Certain situations are more hazardous because parents may not realize the additional potential for injuries.

- Older siblings often leave doors ajar and forget "appetizing" collections in multiples' exploration territory.
- Baby-sitters cannot appreciate the exaggerated effect of multiple distractions. Consider hiring two or more and assigning one to a specific toddler or two.
- Visitors' purses often contain medications, matches, and other dangerous items.
- Pools are special attractions. They cannot be childproofed even if covered so a surrounding fence and locked gate are crucial.
- Toddler and preschool multiples face additional dangers. (See Keys 41 and 44.)
- Your multiples' environment is wherever they happen to be. If away from the childproofed home, childproof the new environment. Do not let anyone scoff at or undermine your efforts. Be alert to medications in older persons' homes.

• Special services exist to evaluate homes for hazards and recommend ways to change or use safeguard equipment. This is an important service but it may be affiliated with a specific brand of safety items. For information, look in the yellow pages under "Baby" or "Child" sections. Also some children's hospitals have child safety task forces.

Accidents

Despite your best efforts, one or more might sustain an injury. Be prepared for any possibility.

• Take infant and child cardiopulmonary resuscitation (CPR) and first-aid classes.
• Post the number for the poison control center and emergency help near every phone.
• Have syrup of ipecac available, but talk to someone at the poison control center before using it. Inducing vomiting sometimes causes additional damage.
• Go over safety instructions with anyone who provides care for your children.

Every multiple has the same need as any baby/child to explore the environment. This creates a greater challenge for you, who must keep track of two or more. There is no substitute for a childproofed environment if you wish to avoid a situation that ends with "If only I had . . ."

40

~~~~~~

MOVING INTO TODDLERHOOD

15 TO 36 MONTHS

There is nothing quite like rediscovering the world through a toddler's eye, unless it is rediscovering the world through the eyes of multiple toddlers! Having several times as much to discover may frequently leave parents feeling breathless. Toddler multiples often create situations that result in unique parenting experiences as they head in different directions at once while their multiple-multiple relationships develop at a rapid rate.

Toddler Development

Motor development. Toddlers make great strides in both large (gross) and small (fine) motor development, but each may make greater strides in one area. Parents may become concerned if one multiple is more focused on large motor skills, such as running and climbing, and another concentrates more on small motor development, such as block building. Still, if one appears to lag behind significantly in either aspect of motor development, discuss this concern with the pediatric care provider. Multiples *are* more at risk for developmental delays, especially if they were very premature at birth or were considered very low birth weight.

Socialization. Dealing with a same-age peer means that multiple toddlers operate in a different environment than most single-born toddlers. Unlike single toddlers who tend to play alongside each other but interact very little, which is called "parallel" play, toddler multiples interact a great deal. However, their interactive styles may seem a bit primitive. For this reason, parents often describe their multiples as either "kissing or killing" each other during many of their interactions. This is enhanced or minimized depending on their individual activity levels and motor orientation.

- Multiples often develop a sense of sharing much earlier than other toddlers. Of course, after a few minutes of sharing, they may end up fighting over the item in question!
- Multiples begin to watch out for each other during toddlerhood. One will often make certain that the other(s) has any treat before enjoying her or his own. Also, multiples may fight with each other, but anyone else bothering one multiple is likely to have to contend with the other(s) as well.
- If a parent must punish one multiple for hurting another, the "victim" often becomes more upset than the "aggressor."
- Envy, an emotion not thought to emerge until the preschool years, may be seen earlier with multiples. Each often wants the same thing at the same time, even when more than one of the same item is available so that each may have his or her own.
- Jealousy and envy may give rise to competition between or among members of the set. Toddler multiples may compete for toys, activities, and, perhaps most of all, for *you*. This may lead to individual demands for equal time and attention from parents.
- Children often pair off during play. This may leave someone "out" in odd-numbered sets. The odd one out may shift among members of the set or it may always be the same one.

Language development. Besides typical questions about language development, parents may have multiples-specific language concerns.

Studies indicate that speech delays are slightly more common for twins. Preterm birth and less parental stimulation are considered contributing factors, which only increase as the number of multiples increases. Also, each multiple hears any mispronounced words of the other(s). Applaud each toddler's efforts to speak, ask each questions that encourage verbal responses, and reinforce or properly repeat whatever words and phrases any says.

A multiple who is more verbal or more extroverted often assumes the role of spokesperson. Since each toddler must learn to communicate with words and practicing speech is the way to do this, watch for and avoid letting any multiple take over as the set's representative. For instance, when one answers for another, you might say, "Thank you, (spokesperson's name), but I was asking (silent toddler's name) about this." Then make eye contact with the silent toddler and restate the question.

Idioglossia is the name for the development of a special language by multiples. Although the members of many sets make up and share words for certain items or activities, few create a complete language. In most cases of true idioglossia, the multiples involved were left to entertain each other and had little parental interaction or stimulation.

Multiples' Individuality

Most parents find it easier to think of the individuals within a set of multiples by toddlerhood. They now feel more in tune with, or have differentiated between, both the sharp and the subtle similarities and differences of their multiples. However, the dynamics of the set continues to have an impact on parenting.

- Letting each multiple make simple choices enhances each child's sense of individuality. (See Key 42.)
- Dressing multiples in look-alike clothing may no longer feel "right," yet some parents find themselves compelled to continue. To stop this practice, pick out several mix-and-match clothing items and then let each toddler choose what to wear.
- Each child is incomparable. As you become able to differentiate one child from another, the comparisons made to distinguish one from another should end. *Comparisons* too easily lead to *labeling*, especially if any is easier to manage than the other(s). Also, multiples may still be little but they have big ears. They now will understand any comparative remarks they overhear.
- "Mine" is a favorite word of any toddler, because a toddler is beginning to understand that he or she is a separate person. Thus each multiple should be given exclusive ownership of some clothing and toys. Duplicate items can be initialed, but most multiples quickly learn to identify their own belongings.

- Each toddler may want a few "mine" possessions, but some multiples want any duplicate items to be *exactly* alike. For instance, a parent may spend hours searching for tricycles in different colors or the same doll wearing different outfits only to have multiples fight over the ownership of the same one.
- Finding a moment to spend one-to-one with each toddler may be difficult. As long as one is awake, none of the others is likely to let the first alone with you.
- Many multiples resist even brief separations. Toddlers cannot yet understand the concept of taking turns to go out with a parent. However, a parent may be able to take higher-order multiples along one at a time, since the multiples at home will still have each other.
- Don't become over-concerned regarding dominance or passiveness between or among the members in a set of multiples. There are different kinds of dominance, so one may be physically dominant and another may be mentally dominant. Multiples often flip-flop dominance. Appearing to be passive may simply be an expression of one multiple's easy-going nature rather than the mark of someone who is too easily influenced by others.
- Flip-flopping may occur less frequently but may last longer than in multiples' first year. (See Key 21.)
- When toddler twins are on the same wavelength, a third personality may emerge from their combined energy, the "twin" personality. Parents of higher-order multiples might find member combinations that lead to additional multiples-related personalities! So parents may discover there is each individual toddler plus a joint personality (or two).

Multiples' Relationships

Multiples invest a lot of energy in their developing relationship(s) from this point on. The interactions between two multiples, whether twins or pairs within a higher-order set, or among the entire set of higher-order multiples, form the basis for their relationship(s). They are working on that relationship as they cooperate, compete, share, and fight. Parents will not, and need not, always agree with their methods. Still, multiples have a right to their own relationship(s), and they must work this out for themselves.

41

COMBINED ENERGY

Multiples may be off and running, but not all move at the same speed. Whether multiples "walk" or "race" through the toddler years depends on each one's inborn activity level and motor orientation, and how each multiple's level combines with the other(s). It's the combination of individual levels that often influences parents' experiences during this stage.

A *walker* tends be an observer, letting others bring the world to her or him. A *jogger* moves faster and explores whatever is available in the easily reached vicinity. A *racer* is constantly moving and will go up, over, around, and through for the sheer thrill or to procure any object he or she considers worthy. A multiple possessed of a higher activity level often influences another moving at a slower pace, and together their pace is faster still.

Identical multiples are more likely than fraternal ones to share similar activity levels, since activity level has a genetic component. Multiples of different genders tend to be the most diverse.

Significance of Pace

The higher the multiples' combined level of activity, the more challenging it becomes for parents to stay one step ahead of them.

Parents may wonder if their racers or racer-jogger combinations are hyperactive. Usually it is multiples' combined energy that makes them more difficult. For clues about hyperactivity, watch to see if each toddler acts differently and is easier to manage when alone.

Dramatic childproofing is needed if two or more racers are in a household. Parents of walkers may have to be careful they don't become too complacent. Any toddler can get into potentially dangerous situations even when it's rare for him to seek them out.

Toddlerproofing for Multiples

Parents find that "two heads *are* better than one" when multiples dream up schemes that few single toddlers could imagine, much less implement. There is *nothing* that multiple racers or joggers cannot and will not get into when working in tandem. Together they can drag a chair to climb to something out of reach. If each takes a drawer pull, they can see what is inside or use the drawers as steps. New "tricks" are quickly taught to the other(s). Any trick can then be used by each when apart from the other(s). These childproofing suggestions can be used with those of Key 39.

- Household items moved earlier should be placed even higher or stored somewhere that toddlers can't go.
- Kitchen appliances pose special problems. Parents of multiples have capped stove knobs, used bungee cords to keep oven and refrigerator doors closed, and even padlocked the refrigerator.
- Keep knives, scissors, matches, and other unsafe items in a chest with a lock. Use a second locked chest for medications or vitamins.
- Furniture posing a safety hazard is better off if moved or stored. These might include items with sharp edges or corners, or pieces that can be used for climbing, such as lightweight dining chairs that two toddlers can shift to another spot and use to reach someplace higher. Some parents substitute folding chairs at meals. Afterward the chairs are folded and stowed flat on top of the table so they are unavailable for climbing.
- Once a child learns to climb out of a crib, that multiple often teaches the new skill to the other(s). Placing a firm mattress on the floor may produce a safer sleeping arrangement for multiples. Or mesh domes can be attached over the toddlers' cribs. If used, these domes should still allow toddlers to stand, and the dome should be removed if it is distressful to the child.
- If multiples climb, pull items out of drawers, or tear down curtains, their bedroom can be stripped of furniture, window treatments, wall hangings, and so on. All they really need is their bed(s) or a mattress. Gate or use a half-door for the bedroom door. Higher baby gates are available: Multiples have been

167

known to stack pillows to climb over standard-size gates. Some parents separate multiples in different bedrooms, but this is not always feasible. Plus, many multiples sleep better when together.

- Check how far windows open, that they lock well, and that screens are well secured. To avoid climbs out of windows, beds or a mattress should not be underneath or next to a window.

- Slide locks can be placed on the outside of bedroom, bathroom, or other doors to prevent multiples from exploring rooms without a parent's supervision. These locks should be fastened so they are too high for multiples to reach but accessible for an older child or an adult. Hook-and-eye locks are less effective, as agile multiples quickly figure how to open them.

- Securely block balconies and outside decks. Be certain the blocking mechanism does not provide a toehold for climbing and that a child cannot entrap a limb or head in the material.

- Childproof the yard and garage. Lawn tools or equipment and poisonous materials, such as pesticides, should be locked away with every use. Enclose pools or fountains with high fencing. Use a padlock or combination lock on the gate.

- If enclosing a grassy area, make certain that materials used and fence height are adequate. When a fence is attached to the house, some parents don't install a gate. Then their multiples' only access beyond the fence is through the house.

- Expect toddler multiples to take off in different directions or for one to run ahead as another slows to inspect every leaf that has fallen in the path. Because of this, supervising two or more toddlers outdoors is more difficult unless they are confined by a fence, in a stroller, or by a harness with a leash/tether.

- Car seats are not optional. All children of any age should be restrained when riding in a car to protect them from injury and to minimize distractions for the driver. If any multiple learns to get out of a car-seat restraining device, pull over, stop the car, and reapply the device. Repeat this action until the child learns that no one goes "bye-bye" unless seat belts are in place. Without immediate action, figure that one multiple will soon teach the other(s) how to get out of a car-seat belt.

Energy-Diverting Play

Providing a diversion to redirect multiples' energy often diffuses potentially dangerous or mischievous behaviors. However, not all toys are "multiples-proof"! Multiples often discover new or creative uses for toys, so the toy that may be perfect for a single child becomes unsafe in the hands of two or more playing with it. Also, some toys cannot stand up to the wear and tear of multiple users. Consider the following when purchasing toys:

- *Any* toy, or its pieces, can become an unintentional weapon when one multiple throws or uses it to hit another. To minimize risk, check all toys for weight and sharp edges or points.
- Because active multiples tend to be "harder" on toys, poorly constructed toys rarely last long. Also, toys with numerous pieces are impossible to keep together.
- Toys that encourage gross motor development are a favorite of racers and joggers, so *durable* indoor and outdoor gym equipment is an excellent investment. A small, indoor/outdoor teeter-totter/seesaw must have been made with multiples in mind!
- Multiples of all activity levels usually are fascinated by:

    1. a large cardboard box
    2. supervised water play—indoors or out
    3. blocks—rubber ones are safer
    4. push-pull toys
    5. sturdy, one-piece bead and block loops (beads or blocks slide over roller-coaster-shaped wires on a wood base).
- *You* continue to be your multiples' most irreplaceable and fun toy. Get on the floor and act as a human jungle gym by letting them crawl on you. Read to them daily; let each choose stories.

Can You Top This?

No one has more entertaining or hilarious toddler stories than a parent relating the antics of active multiples. Don't be surprised if you become a popular storyteller wherever parents gather. Who knows? If you write them all down, you may even find you have a comedy act you can take on the road—after your multiples have gone on to the calmer preschool age, of course!

42

DISCIPLINE

D iscipline is about guidance. When parents discipline, they guide a child toward the kind of behavior that is acceptable for a society. Multiples' interactions lead to unique behaviors that sometimes make it more of a challenge to provide the guidance they need. Unlike a single child, one of multiples often is more interested in pleasing the other(s) than in pleasing Mom or Dad. After all, a same-age multiple always has more exciting ideas about "fun" behavior than their parents.

No!

Toddler multiples are likely to hear the word "no" much more often than a single toddler. Every multiple hears the "no" meant for that individual multiple, the ones meant for each other multiple, the ones said in response to the mischief they get into together, and the ones for all those extra schemes that only multiples can devise and actually carry out. Parents can eliminate having to say the word "no" as often when they

- have realistic expectations for toddlers' behavior—not only expectations which are realistic for the multiples' age and stage of development but also expectations that take into account each child's behavioral style.
- childproof thoroughly so there are fewer dangerous or mischievous situations just waiting to happen. (See Keys 39 and 40 for multiples-specific childproofing ideas.)
- become sensitive to and anticipate each one's individual sleep and hunger needs. Negative behavior often is associated with a child who is overtired or hungry.
- decrease any multiple's need to gain a parent's attention through negative behavior by giving each child lots of hugs, kisses, and

backrubs, and by reinforcing positive behavior, such as when two or more multiples share a toy or cooperate on a parent-approved endeavor. A more-difficult-to-manage multiple may need lots and lots of positive reinforcement and parental reassurance.

• don't describe their multiples' escapades to others if there is even a remote chance that one of the multiples might hear. Relating such stories within any multiple's hearing only encourages further mischief making.

Fighting

Fighting between two or more multiples is a common occurrence for many sets, but toddlers do not fight fair. They are too young to comprehend that hitting, pushing, or pulling on another can result in injury. Also, many parents of multiples have had to cope with one multiple who bites another when frustrated.

Avoid interfering immediately when multiples fight, unless any child is in imminent danger. Instead, observe from a distance. There are a number of reasons to stand back.

• Parents sometimes are surprised to discover an apparent "victim" instigating many fights, purposefully goading another until that multiple lashes out.

• Intervention can result in "taking sides" unfairly. Parents often miss the breakout phase of a fight, so they may not see what triggered a disagreement or who initiated the action.

• Quick intervention often leads to more fighting instead of less because of the attention received as a result. The amount of fighting often declines when parents seem to ignore multiples' fights.

• There are many ways to "win" a fight. Not all alleged "victims" mind dealing with a more aggressive multiple by moving out of the way or giving up a toy for a while.

• When a parent always "rescues" a victim, multiples cannot learn how to settle conflicts with one another. Ultimately, multiples must develop their own "rules" to guide any relationship(s) between members of the set, and sometimes fighting plays a role in rules' creation. (See the section on multiples' relationships in Key 40.)

When parents avoid "rescue" action at the first sign of a disagreement, it does not mean they should condone inappropriate behavior or fail to intervene if the fighting escalates and any child is in danger of being hurt. When intervention is necessary, some parental actions are more likely to be effective.

- Isolating the "aggressor" from the "victim" for a few minutes tends to be the *most effective* intervention, as most toddler multiples do not like to be separated. (A few minutes is a long time to a toddler. Time apart can be increased as they grow older.)
- Physical punishment tends to be the *least effective* method for dealing with any multiple's physically aggressive behavior. A young child cannot distinguish being told, "Don't hit or bite your brother (sister)," with then being spanked (hit) or bitten in response to doing those very actions. This strategy only reinforces the behavior a parent wants to stop. It also gives children the impression that one who is bigger or tougher may physically intimidate a smaller or weaker multiple.
- In *simple* terms, label inappropriate behaviors and the feeling that often accompanies such behavior, and then suggest alternate behaviors. An example might go something like this, "You seem very angry with your brother, and when someone's angry he may feel like hitting, but hit the punching bag instead of the person." (Parents probably will repeat this strategy numerous times and in numerous variations as multiples grow!)
- When a toy is the focus of a fight, the toy's owner might be given the authority to decide whether another may play with it, which usually provides a parent with an opportunity for a simple discussion about sharing. A jointly owned toy may require a "toy time out" on a shelf for several minutes if its owners cannot take turns playing with it. Repeat "toy time out" when fights recur or shelve the toy for the rest of that day if it continues to cause a sharing problem.

Other Discipline Issues

Discipline strategies that work well for a single toddler, such as diverting one's attention or substituting a toy with another, may be completely undermined by multiples' interactions. A diversion or substitute can easily become the sources of new mischief or bickering.

Parents often are unsure whether an individual or all multiples were involved in mischief. When parents ask which child was involved, each points to another to say, "She did it."

Toddler multiples quickly learn to split up and run in different directions. They realize parents can't run after more than one at once.

Parents find some forms of guidance work better with multiples than others:

- A traditional *time out* in a nearby chair may be ineffective when a "free" multiple entertains a "captive" one. Facing the time-out chair to the wall or isolating the one requiring punishment in his room often is more effective. Five minutes or less is long enough for toddler time outs.
- Think twice about punishing everyone in the set unless certain that every multiple was involved in the misbehavior. Collective punishment is unfair to any multiple who was an "innocent bystander." Label the inappropriate behavior and suggest alternative behavior if unsure which multiple was involved. When multiples are observed creating mischief collectively, however, each should share in the consequences, even if a parent has to track all of them down after they've run in different directions.
- Letting each multiple make choices often cuts down on inappropriate behaviors and defuses many volatile situations, but all options should be agreeable to the parent!
    1. To keep choices simple for toddlers, limit choices to two items. "Do you want to wear a dress or overalls today?" "Would you like cereal or scrambled eggs for breakfast?" Once a choice is made, do not give in to changes of mind.

Although this often occurs when multiples choose different options, all must learn to live with the consequences of choice.

2. Sometimes a toddler's wishes conflict with what must be done. Then the choice will focus on "how" rather than "what" is to be done. "Do you want to get into your car seat on your own, or do you want me to put you in it?" "Can you share the blocks or shall I put them on the toy 'time-out' shelf?"

3. When any multiple refuses to make a choice, repeat the options once and tell the child you will be making the choice if she can't decide within a specified time limit. Be sure to follow through with the choice if the child still doesn't make it. Learning that refusing to choose is a choice in itself is a valuable lesson for a child.

Threatening any or all multiples with unrealistic punishment that cannot be carried out will not improve their behavior. Unrealistic punishments are unfair. Not following through with a punishment encourages them to break rules and teaches them that you don't really mean what you say.

The Importance of Parents

Active and bright multiples sometimes wear their parents down until parents "give up" and let them get away with inappropriate behavior. No one "wins" when this happens. (Everyone gives up on occasion. Start over later in the day or tomorrow.)

Toddler multiples have a right to consistent discipline, so they'll remain safe and learn how to behave properly. They need parents' guidance. Teaching self-control to toddler multiples requires a major investment of parents' time and effort. Fortunately, or unfortunately for those who give up or give in too often, parents often find they continue to use the basic discipline strategies they develop at this stage through multiples' adolescence.

43

TOILET LEARNING

W hat parent of multiples does not look forward to eliminating a mountain of diapers? It may be tempting, but trying to speed toilet training often has the opposite effect. It may prolong the process and result in frustration for both parents and multiples. Teaching individual multiples to use the toilet is a quick and easy process *when* they are ready.

Ready or Not?

No child can consistently control the muscles used for bowel or bladder function before 18 months, and this control may occur as late as three years. Mental readiness, or interest, does not always coincide with physical readiness to use the toilet. Although they may not say it in so many words, a child will let parents know when she or he wants to begin using the toilet. Parents cannot go wrong when they let their multiples be their guides.

An individual multiple may be saying it's time to introduce the potty chair when he or she shows a growing interest in a parent's use of the toilet, wants to be changed immediately after wetting or soiling a diaper, or often wakes up dry after napping.

Girls tend to be ready earlier than boys. Parents with boy-girl sets often find one is out of diapers months before another.

Identical multiples are often ready at about the same time. Same-sex fraternal multiples may be on similar or different timetables.

Teaching Multiples

There are advantages and disadvantages to introducing toilet training to multiples separately versus together. Teaching each separately may be less confusing but the process may seem prolonged. Teaching two or three at once means parents will have to deal with at least twice as many accidents, but the process may be completed in a shorter period. Parents don't always have the option of making this decision. Often multiples make it for them.

- When one is ready before another, some parents wait until both or all are ready before introducing the potty to any. It's better to move ahead, however, if one really wants to try *now*.
- Competitive members in a set often inspire one another. The last to learn will not like another using the toilet when she cannot.
- Sitting on potty chairs can become "party time" for multiples. Leave potty chairs in the bathroom, so everyone will associate that room with going on the toilet. Never make any child sit on the potty chair when he signals he wants off. Sitting on the potty for ten minutes or longer without going to the bathroom indicates that the child doesn't get the idea yet. If ready and interested, most use the potty within minutes of sitting down.
- Offering an incentive encourages some multiples to progress, but keep it low key so any multiple who is not yet ready will not feel bad. An incentive combined with the competitiveness of some multiples can be truly motivational!
- If any child does not seem to be getting the idea or has many accidents after a week, ask him if he would like to wear diapers a while longer. Relax, and try again in a few weeks or months.

Helps and Hindrances

- Superabsorbent disposable diapers or panties seem to work too well at keeping toddlers dry, so multiples may not know, or care, that their diapers are wet. Switching to less absorbent diapers for daytime use sometimes speeds toilet training.
- Although toddlers or preschoolers may be anxious to wear the fancy underwear with the ballerinas or superheroes on them, training pants absorb accidents better. Knowing that "big kid" underwear is waiting is an incentive for some multiples.
- If available, a diaper service can supply training pants.
- Overalls and pants with zippers, snaps, or buttons are a hindrance when any toddler has to go to the bathroom *now*. Dresses or T-shirts worn with training pants alone are best dur-

ing the actual training process. Pants with elastic waistbands are easier to manipulate once any multiple regularly uses the toilet.

- It is easier to let multiples run around wearing only a T-shirt and training pants if toilet training is initiated during warmer weather.

Potty-Chairs

Many parents wonder if they will need one potty-chair or one for each multiple. It depends on how many are ready at once and how old they are when toilet learning begins.

- If two are likely to use the toilet at the same time, two potty-chairs are necessary. Usually, two multiples can share one chair. At first, put one toddler on the potty-chair after another. Later, multiples should rarely have to use the toilet at the same time.
- The younger multiples are when toilet learning begins, the more likely they are to prefer small, low-to-the-ground potty-chairs.
- Older toddler and preschool multiples may prefer the "big potty." A one-step stool makes this easier to accomplish.
- Some multiples may feel more comfortable using a potty seat that fits over an adult toilet seat. Having this type of seat available may solve a "two potty-chair" dilemma.
- Boys may want to stand facing the toilet like Daddy as soon as possible. (The girl of boy-girl sets may try to emulate her brother!)

A Positive Attitude Is the Key

Learning to use the toilet is a big step, and everyone profits when parents remain relaxed. Although potty training does not take long when any multiple is ready, it rarely happens in one day.

- Expect accidents and handle them nonchalantly.
- Ignore advice that does not meet any child's needs. You can introduce the toilet, but no one can make a child use it. This is a physical function each child must be ready and willing to master.
- If any are not ready, don't make a big deal of it. Each will be ready eventually. Really! Look on the bright side. Parents of "early learner" multiples are undoubtedly making frequent stops at every rest room they come to when on outings. There are advantages to everything, even prolonged double or triple diaper duty!

44

~~~~~~

PRESCHOOL

THREE YEARS TO KINDERGARTEN

Each preschool multiple's horizons expand beyond the other members of the set, the family, and the home. Multiples now become part of a larger community. It is time to meet new friends and, possibly, begin attending school.

Growth and Development

Multiples will make great strides in their intellectual, or cognitive, abilities at this age. Although their basic activity levels do not change, new energy outlets become available.

- "Let's pretend" usually becomes multiples' favorite phrase. Be sure to eavesdrop on their imaginary play. Together multiples concoct extraspecial scenarios.
- Preschoolers like to do things for themselves. Multiples may dress themselves earlier since they are able to help each other.
- "Taking turns" finally has meaning. Separate outings for parents with each child are real treats. Devise a system to keep track of whose turn it is to avoid unnecessary arguments or hurt feelings.
- Taking turns sinks in *so* well it is applied to many things: who sits next to a parent, who pushes the elevator button, who chooses the TV show, and so on.
- "Potty" words are a brief hit with most preschoolers, but this phase often lingers for multiples. A single preschooler receives little positive feedback, but multiples laugh hysterically at each other, providing reinforcement for this behavior.
- The combined energy of some sets still results in a "group" personality. Its form often alters as multiples spend more time outside the home. It might make fewer appearances than before, but when it appears it may be intense. Parents may be able to "feel"

energy building between/among multiples as they work them-selves into a "tizzy." In the midst of this they are oblivious to everything but each other.

• Often any girl in a set of opposite-sex multiples "mothers" her brother(s) because girls generally are somewhat ahead developmentally.

Preschool and Kindergarten Decisions

Parents of multiples have different concerns than parents of single children. Read Key 45 in conjunction with this section.

If considering preschool for multiples, observe and evaluate programs to find one that suits your philosophy and each child's needs.

To spend time alone with each child, some parents send their multiples to preschool or kindergarten on separate days, or they send one or two for the morning session and another one or two in the afternoon. Most parents send multiples together and enjoy a few free hours to themselves—finally!

Multiples, especially competitive ones, sometimes work better for someone other than a parent, but preschool is not a necessity. Other options are to work with each or form a play group with other parents.

New Friends

Although "real" play is nothing new for multiples, it is for many of the children they meet. Multiples apply strategies learned for dealing with each other to new friendships. In turn, new friend-ships affect the multiples' relationship.

• Preschool may not offer enough play experiences with other children. "Import" children into your home to play.
• Children seem to play best when there are even numbers, as they usually break into pairs.
• Some multiples ignore a new playmate, but frequently one multi-ple is excluded from play. This can be a shock for a multiple who always has had a built-in playmate.

- Multiples are so tuned to one another that they may be surprised when other children do not respond in the "right" way, which is as the other members of the set would.
- Some new playmates feel overwhelmed facing twins, triplets, or more and play only with one. This is especially true if multiples dress alike and approach another child as a united front. However, other children are intrigued by multiples.
- Most children can distinguish between identical or similar looking multiples quickly, even when many adults cannot.

Toys

Buying toys for a group of children the same age is more complicated than buying toys for one.

Many multiples want the same toys. Sometimes each asks for something different, but they get upset when any of them do not have what the other(s) has. If this becomes a predictable pattern, discuss possible feelings ahead of time. Buy each the same thing if it seems appropriate. This eventually changes.

Multiples should not have to share toys, such as bikes or dolls. A few books, puzzles, or plastic building block sets also should be privately owned.

Big items, like a sandbox, play table, small pool, pretend kitchen, gym set, doll house, race track/garage, or big block set, can usually be shared.

Preschool Childproofing

Preschool multiples still require supervision as they interact.

- "Tizzy" multiples need more supervision. They easily get carried away, which can lead to hazardous situations.
- Preschool multiples can mix fantasy and reality in a dangerous way. They might combine play cooking with real cooking appliances. Sticks and other objects suddenly become swords or medical thermometers to use on one another.
- Preschool multiples may encourage one another to sample harmful substances or experiment with matches.

- Supervise joint art time, or their projects may extend to walls, floors, or other surfaces.
- Keep active multiples closer to you by using wrist cuffs with leashes when out with them.

You and Your Multiples

As each multiple adds new friendships and activities outside the home, your relationship with each child changes. There is more time to spend with one child alone.

You still are your multiples' best developmental toy. Become sensitive to each one's learning style and take advantage of opportunities for promoting individual development.

It is time to let go of dressing multiples alike every day. Clothing choices should belong to each child. Even at this age, when drawers are still filled with duplicate items, multiples often express their individuality by choosing different styles. Other sets love wearing look-alike clothing.

Initially it is heartbreaking when any multiple is rejected by a new friend. How do parents respond? It can be beneficial for each child to be alone for awhile, just as it is beneficial for each to play separately with another child. If you take this in stride, the multiples are more likely to accept the situation, too. At first, sympathize with the one left behind and enjoy one-on-one time with that child. Often a preference for one child flip-flops—a child might play with one multiple this week and another next week.

The Payoff Period

Most parents feel they have entered the payoff period during multiples' preschool years. Although multiples-specific situations still arise, the difficult aspects of parenting multiples diminish and the pleasurable aspects persist. It is a joy to watch multiples begin to soar, separately and together.

45

~~~~~~

SCHOOL: TOGETHER OR SEPARATE?

Any school separation decision *must* be based on the parents' knowledge and understanding of each multiple. It is not a lifelong decision. The multiples' relationship and their classroom needs may change from year to year. A parent must respond to the needs of each child by taking their relationship, learning styles, and the general makeup of the class into account.

When there are options, multiples should have some say about their preferences. Talk to each child separately. Sometimes one prefers separation and another wants to stay together. Total separation may not be an option with higher-order multiples, and parents should choose who is in class with whom and with what teacher. As their parents, the final word should be yours.

Preschool or Kindergarten
The first day of preschool or kindergarten often marks multiples' first separation from their mother. Asking them to separate from each other, too, may be more than they can handle. Many single children settle in more comfortably when in a class with their best friend. In the case of multiples, the best friend(s) just happens to be the other member(s) of the set. Arbitrarily separating multiples may deny them the security that others in the class are allowed.

Grade School
Multiples and circumstances change. Reexamine class placement decision(s) yearly. Teachers and administrators may have input, but the final decision should be the parents'. Arbitrary school policies are inappropriate. Evidence indicates multiples can do well together or apart. Their different learning styles, degree of

competitiveness and independence from one another, and overall class makeup should *all* have an impact on this decision.

The Decision

Evaluate the following when making a placement decision.

No one can force children to be independent. Separation is very difficult for multiples not yet ready for independence.

Nursery school classes are often grouped according to birthdays. If multiples are separated, will some be in a class with children either older or younger?

There are degrees of separation.

1. How much time do kindergarten and first-grade classes spend with each other? Many share story time, snack time, and recess, so separated multiples may still see each other often.
2. If multiples are in the same classroom, they may be in different work groups and spend little time together.
3. Are children from a specific geographic area placed in one classroom? If so, and multiples are separated, one will be with known peers and another will be with strangers.
4. Does separating multiples mean that one must go in the morning and another in the afternoon?

Interview potential teachers. If they communicate often and are sensitive to your concerns about separation, they will work with you to ensure the success of the placement.

If you separate multiples in kindergarten, also choose who goes to which class. Ask to see the class list shortly before school starts, and look for which friends are in each class.

Even if everyone wants separation, it still is a tremendous adjustment. Give each time to work it out.

Working with School Officials

Some school systems have arbitrary rules about separating multiples. Of those with a policy, most insist on separation. The assumption is that multiples develop better as individuals and are more successful in school if separated. Research doesn't support this. Arbitrary policies for separation deny individuality as much as insisting they stay together when they are ready for separate experiences.

If you are at odds with the administration, note the following:

- Do not discuss separation in front of the multiples. This puts parents in a win-or-lose situation with the administration. Once this issue is resolved, you will want your children to know that you and the school staff are on the same side.
- State your case clearly and unemotionally. Be assertive, not aggressive.
- Ask to see any separation policy in writing. It is unlikely that an administrator will be able to produce any documentation to support a school policy on separation. Administrators are often surprised to discover that what they thought was school policy is actually just "the way it has always been done."
- If there is a written policy, ask why it was adopted. Often someone thought it was a good idea and passed a resolution without giving it thought. If an administrator claims the policy is based on research evidence, ask to see research; if the administrator claims it is based on "our experience," ask for a documented comparison of multiples separated and left together.
- Don't consider separation because it is thought to be "easier" for a teacher. Schools are supposed to meet children's needs, not educators', and some multiples learn best when together.
- Remind school officials that this year's decision is not a lifelong one. Ask them to place your multiples as you think they should be for a period of time. If it does not work out, they can be switched later. This should work both ways. The school should be willing to change if their decision is not working.

Consequences

If multiples appear to be happy in their school situation, then the right decision has been made. Have confidence in yourself and your own judgment about what is best for your children.

46

~~~~~~

THE EARLY ELEMENTARY YEARS

Multiples begin to truly explore their relationship during the early elementary school years. People outside the family increasingly influence how each sees the other. As they are exposed to new ideas and activities, opportunities for individual expression expand.

Growth and Development

Parents might notice a shift in multiples' relationships as each becomes more aware of himself as an individual.

Multiples may begin to express interest in extracurricular activities. It usually is best to let each choose her own activities. Sometimes they may want to try the same activity and other times each might want to do something different. Being part of a set should not influence activity options. Also every member should not have to do the same thing because it is more convenient for parents.

Other children, and even adults, often have stereotypical images and expectations about multiples. They may think fraternal multiples would not choose any of the same activities because they are not "real" multiples since they do not look alike or are different genders. Identicals are supposed to look and act alike and want to do all the same things. Others may insist on labeling multiples, even higher-order multiples, as "the smart one," "the pretty one," "the athlete," "the leader." For the first time, the multiples may confront set-related situations or stereotypes without a parent to run interference. They will learn to handle these situations, but your suggestions might be helpful.

185

One or more multiples may resent being called by the "wrong" name, although most prefer this to someone yelling, "Hey, twin" or "Hey, you." Explain to multiples that other people may forget which name goes with which face. Advise multiples that they can tell others to call them by name but that frequent reminders may be necessary.

School-age children are probably ready for a *simple* explanation of how multiples develop from one, two, or more eggs. (See Key 1.) Descriptive drawings help. Expand on the explanation as they grow.

Multiples learn to take advantage of their celebrity without any encouragement from parents!

Multiples this age seem to really love, hate, *or* both love and hate each other. Same-sex girl sets, especially identical girls, are more likely to emphasize the twin bond. The love-hate relationship seems more in evidence with all-boy sets, or perhaps their ambivalent behaviors tend to be more obvious.

One or all sometimes may say they wish they were not part of a set. They may call each other "ugly," which is particularly amusing if they happen to be identical twins! None is rejecting their relationship, they simply desire to be recognized as individuals.

Competition may increase as multiples "look over each other's shoulders" at schoolwork, report cards, or achievements in extracurricular activities. One may be very upset when another learns something first, whether it is a math concept or how to ride a two-wheeled bicycle.

As with other behaviors, learning styles are influenced by twin type. Fraternal multiples are more likely to have different learning styles, especially girl-boy sets. Identical ones usually have more similar styles. Differences *and* similarities can lead to comparisons and competition *or* cooperation in the form of studying and helping one another.

School

Multiples interact in the school environment for several hours a day. Along with reading and math lessons, they learn a great deal about themselves and others.

- Teachers can also have stereotypical attitudes about multiples. It is the parents' job to help teachers perceive the members of a set of multiples as individuals. At the beginning of each school year, discuss with them each one's strengths and weaknesses and differences and similarities.
- Evaluate each multiple's learning style separately. All want to do well and please you. Parents whose multiples were premature or had difficulties during pregnancy or at birth should be somewhat more alert for signs of learning difficulties and disabilities. Also, males are more likely to be affected. Pursue testing when any of them experiences great difficulty.
- Make separate appointments for each one's parent-teacher conference, as you need to talk about each one individually. If multiples are in separate classrooms, ask each teacher how "her" child is doing in that particular classroom, with this teacher, and these children. Avoid mentioning another's name unless you are asking something specific about their relationship.
- If multiples are in the same classroom, first discuss each child's progress separately. Then ask how they relate during the school day. You need to know if any of them withdraw rather than compete with the other(s), or if one always answers for the group or another. You will not want this to be the focus of the conference, however, so get back on track if you or the teacher digress to "set" talk.
- More parents are becoming interested in home-schooling their multiples. Many networks now exist to help parents. For information, check the Yellow Pages, your local library, and search the Internet. Also see Appendix B: Resource—Home-Schooling Multiples.

Friendships

Peer relationships become a priority during the elementary school years.

Children this age often view friendships with members of the opposite sex with disgust. Obviously, this can have a tremendous impact for girl-boy multiple sets. Some may identify more with same-sex peers or a sibling of the same sex. This is a part of the development of their relationship.

Multiples often have both shared and separate friendships. It is up to you to let other parents know your thoughts concerning separate or joint invitations for birthday parties or overnight stays. Even though one may feel hurt at the time, do you allow them to have these separate experiences, or do you insist that all or none be invited? Parents' decisions about such invitations can reinforce the set or reinforce individuals. Generally, the number of separate invitations evens out. (See Key 44.)

You and Your Multiples

Your multiples' relationship always belongs to them, and they must develop it for themselves. Parents can support and encourage them as they explore their differences and similarities, but you cannot do the work for them. Share your values about cooperation and competition. Avoid comparisons by reinforcing each one's strengths while helping each work on weaker areas. Step back and let each learn to handle any difficulties that arise between or among themselves, other siblings, and peers. Your multiples' world may be expanding, but your position as their most crucial developmental "toy" does not.

47

SPECIAL SITUATIONS

When Any of a Multiple Set Is Physically or Mentally Impaired

Multiples are affected by physical or mental impairments slightly more often than single-born children. Impairments may be associated with congenital (inborn) problems, uterine conditions, or pregnancy and birth complications. Even when intervention eventually leads to resolution of the health problem, caring for an impaired baby or child requires extra parental time at home and for health-care intervention. The additional work and anxiety about any multiple's condition can add to the level of stress parents of multiples already experience.

If any multiple is affected by an impairment, it may influence the formation of an attachment with that baby. A deeper bond may develop sooner when a parent must spend extra time caring for a particular baby. However, it may take longer to form an attachment with a real but "imperfect" baby, as it takes time to grieve the loss of a "perfect" fantasy baby. The presence of a "perfect" multiple(s) complicates the process. In many instances, the perfect multiple(s) also was initially more responsive after birth, so a relationship(s) naturally developed with the one(s) who were able to interact earlier.

Of course, any difficulty in forming an attachment must be overcome, as an impairing condition does not negate a baby's need for and right to a strong relationship with each parent. Perhaps more than the other(s), this multiple will depend on parental relationships recognizing and fostering his strengths while accepting yet minimizing any weaknesses.

Hospitalization of Any Multiple

Hospitalizing one multiple affects the other(s), because the multiple requiring hospital treatment usually has the most need for a parent's presence. Although that one's needs take precedence, each multiple still needs frequent "in person" interaction with parents. Parents, especially the primary caregiver parent, often feel torn when one multiple requires hospitalization during infancy or early childhood.

There are times when hospitalization is optional, or elective, and when treatment can be safely delayed. Occasionally, hospitalization for a medical procedure or treatment is preferred by the care provider yet it can be done safely in another setting. For those situations, a care provider may be willing to postpone treatment or use an outpatient setting once the circumstances are explained.

When hospitalization is unavoidable, parents have worked out all sorts of arrangements with a hospital. Some take a twin or second multiple with them and all room-in with the hospitalized baby, which is especially helpful if the multiples are being breastfed. This usually requires cooperation between parents and the hospital staff, but the babies often derive comfort from the presence of the other and mothers often feel less torn.

Other parents arrange for the other multiple(s) to visit both the hospitalized multiple and the parent staying with her. Some children's hospitals have special residences for patients' families, but these tend to be for situations requiring long hospital stays far from a family's home.

Parents will want to take turns or ask another familiar adult to briefly sit with the hospitalized child, so they can spend time with the other multiples during a quick trip home or when someone brings the other(s) over to "visit" the parent staying at the hospital. When all multiples cannot room-in during the hospitalization of one, breastfeeding mothers will want to have a hospital-grade, electric breast pump available to maintain milk production for all multiples.

Most hospitals have relaxed visitor policies, which is helpful if any older multiple requires a hospital stay. Sometimes a hospital administration has bent the rules and made exceptions for multiples when one is sick but child visitors aren't allowed.

Multiples share close bonds, and each will need to be reassured that the other is all right. The one(s) at home can easily imagine the hospitalized child's condition is worse than reality. Taking "instant" photos of the one(s) at home and the one in the hospital that can be exchanged and frequent phone calls, even if it's long distance, can help multiples deal with the hospitalization of one.

Single Parents

Being single does not mean a parent of multiples should think she/he must do everything for every baby or child. Parenting multiples often is a monumental task for two-parent families. Single parents with multiples will be more in need of outside sources of physical and emotional support. As with other parents of multiples, single parents benefit from a support network that includes other single parents of multiples. (See Key 30.)

Social service agencies often are aware of other sources of help for the single parent when the type of help needed is not readily available. A single parent of multiples sometimes qualifies for a type of help that would be unavailable to a parent with a single-born child.

Dealing with the Death of a Multiple

There is such excitement and anticipation generated by the expectation of multiple infants. Yet fetal and infant death are higher among multiples because of related complications. When any multiple dies during pregnancy or after birth, a parent experiences the grief of losing a unique and precious baby and also the loss of the set of multiples—"the twins," "the triplets," "the quadruplets," and so on.

The grieving process takes time. Sometimes professional help is needed. There also are support networks for parents who have lost a multiple through death. (See Appendix B: Resources, Grief Support.)

Fetal or Neonatal Death of a Multiple

The death of a multiple during pregnancy or during early infancy may interfere with the formation of an attachment with any surviving multiple(s). It is difficult to simultaneously attach to any survivor(s) and detach from any that die. Most parents say they focus on first forming an attachment with any survivor(s). These parents "postpone" the process of grieving for the multiple that died while bonding with the living multiple(s), although they still describe being overtaken by overwhelming grief off and on.

The loss of any baby is devastating, and relatives and friends may not be able to look a grieving parent in the eye or know what to say to offer comfort. Sometimes thoughtless persons say the wrong thing, such as "Well, at least you have one healthy baby," as if that should be enough. The death of any multiple in the set is an unacceptable loss. The fact that a parent rejoices in the living multiple(s), should not diminish or trivialize the life and subsequent death of another multiple. The parents' grief would not be greater if this had been a single-born infant who had died.

When an Older Multiple Dies

The death of a multiple during childhood forces a parent to deal with the loss of a beloved child, the loss of identity as a set for parent and surviving multiple(s), and the devastating effect on the surviving multiple(s). Other siblings of the child will also grieve, but the grief for any surviving multiple(s) usually is more intense. Parents have to guide the surviving multiple(s) and other siblings through a horrendous period when their own inner resources are depleted from coping with the magnitude of a child's death. In addition to grief support resources for parents, there are resources available for surviving multiples and for children coping with death. (See Appendix B: Resources, Grief Support.)

QUESTIONS AND ANSWERS

My obstetrician refers to my multiple pregnancy as "high risk." Does this mean that there probably will be something wrong with my babies?

Absolutely not! Many expectant parents are frightened by this term. It simply means the potential for developing a pregnancy or birth complication is higher than if you were expecting a single baby. Now that you are expecting multiples, your obstetrician monitors your pregnancy more closely to be prepared for any complication should one arise. Do not allow the potential for complications to cloud your enjoyment and excitement in your pregnancy, however, as many twins and triplets arrive after uncomplicated pregnancies and deliveries. Risk increases as more babies are carried, but with closer medical supervision many women are carrying higher-order multiples longer than ever. Also, advances in NICU care are resulting in better outcomes for babies.

My mother-in-law says that all twins are born early and there is nothing I can do about it. Is she right?

Although 50% of twins are born before 37 weeks of pregnancy, the week considered the cutoff for prematurity, the average length for twin pregnancy is 36.2 weeks. (That "average" decreases by about three weeks for each additional multiple.) Many twins are carried to full term and have weights that are considered good even for single babies. Proper prenatal care with close supervision and a good diet during multiple pregnancy increase the chances of carrying babies to full term or closer to full term, no matter how many multiples a woman is carrying.

My friends say I am more likely to have breastfeeding problems. Is this true?

Multiple babies complicate feedings—no matter how you choose to feed them! If lactation or breast milk expression is initiated soon after birth and is followed by unrestricted breastfeedings or frequent pumpings (8 to 12 within 24 hours) and with correct positioning of the babies at the breast, a mother of multiples is less likely to experience engorgement, sore nipples, or latching difficulties. "Teaching" preterm or sick babies often requires more patience and persistence, but most babies do learn as they become more mature. Delaying or missing a feeding, factors that contribute to plugged ducts and breast infections, can have a greater impact on your greatly increased milk supply. Call a La Leche League leader or a lactation consultant (IBCLC) during your pregnancy to discuss getting off to the best possible breastfeeding start, or call later if you experience a problem or have questions.

Friends and relatives are telling me that I will not be able to breastfeed my multiples because I will not be able to make enough milk. Is that true?

Fortunately, Nature did not forget that women can have more than one baby. Breastfeeding operates on the principle that demand equals supply. Each breastfeeding or breast pumping tells your body to maintain or increase milk production. The more babies you are breastfeeding (or providing milk for) and the more often you breastfeed them or pump, the more milk your body should make. If pumping only, you should obtain between 500 to 1000 ml (cc) (17 to 34 ounces) after 7 to 14 days of about 8 pumping sessions (100 minutes) in 24 hours. You know you have enough breast milk for multiples if each: (1) nurses about 8 to 12 times, (2) soaks 6 to 10 diapers, and (3) has three or more bowel movements every day. Also, each baby should gain about four to eight ounces a week. Contact an IBCLC or a La Leche League leader if you are ever concerned about adequate milk production.

I did not see my premature babies until they were 24 hours old. We missed the bonding that all my friends are talking about. Will I ever love my babies or they love me as much as my friends love theirs?

Yes! Bonding, the formation of an enduring attachment between parent and each baby, is an ongoing process. Bonding with your babies actually begins during pregnancy and continues throughout your lives together. You and your babies have had a challenging start, but you can overcome this setback. It may take some time and effort on your part, but you can come to know, love, and appreciate each as an individual.

My babies came home from the hospital one at a time. Even though I was excited about having multiples and I love them all, I am ashamed to admit that I feel closer to the one who came home first. Is this normal?

Many mothers report feeling closer to the baby they were able to care for first. You had the time and opportunity to get to know that baby alone, but you will never have that luxury after any of the others' homecoming. Do not deny your feelings. Concentrate on responding to and finding one-on-one time with each baby. Eventually, you will feel close to each of them.

I feel so isolated since I had quadruplets. My friends do not have the same problems and concerns as I have. Is there anything I can do?

Recognize that your situation is different from your friends and that many of your concerns are unique to families with multiples. Whether a parent has twins, triplets, quads, or more, your best source for support may be another parent having the same number of multiples with whom you share a similar parenting philosophy and can discuss your set's experiences. Ask your pediatric care provider, Mothers of Multiples Club, or a La Leche League leader for the name of another mother of multiples. You also may log onto the Internet. There are many "parent of multiples" sites that offer question and answer lists or provide chat rooms to help ease the feeling of isolation.

How do I respond to people who say that having twins is the same as having two closely spaced children?

These situations are not the same. People making this comment are usually trying to understand your situation and this seems to be their closest analogy. It is not that one situation is easier or one more difficult. They are simply different.

Parents automatically view and treat children as different individuals when they arrive separately because they get to know the older child before concentrating on the second. Parents of multiples must figure out two or more infants simultaneously.

Even if siblings are separated by only nine months, they are at vastly different stages of growth and development, and these differences influence parents' approaches and the siblings' relationship with one another. It would take two or three years before the behavior of close-in-age siblings might be similar to that of some twins. At that point, similarities often depend on the siblings' temperaments and behavioral styles. Also, a third "twin" personality rarely presents itself between nontwin siblings.

I am considering having another baby. How likely am I to have multiples again?

If your multiples are fraternal (dizygotic) and occurred spontaneously (without assisted reproduction assistance), and there is a history of such fraternal multiples in the female partner's family, chances are this partner inherited a tendency for double or multiple ovulation. Because of this, you are more likely to conceive multiples with subsequent pregnancies than you were with the first multiple pregnancy.

Because the conception of identical (monozygotic) multiples is believed to occur at random, your chances of having a second set of identical multiples are about the same as they were before.

Other factors, such as increasing maternal age and a history of prior pregnancy, also play a role. Those taking ovulatory induction agents or fertility drugs to conceive must ask whether they are taking the same or a different medication. The medication and a woman's sensitivity to it influence the conception of multiples.

My sister told me there is a high incidence of child abuse in families who have multiples. I want these babies, but now I'm worried. What am I supposed to do?

Parenting twins, triplets, or more *is* more stressful than parenting a single child, and some studies have found a higher incidence of abuse among families with multiples. However, abuse is the exception, not the rule, for families of multiples. When it does occur, often one member of the set of multiples or an older sibling is victimized. The behavior tends to follow a particular pattern when abuse involves more than one child.

There are theories about abuse in families with multiples, but research is limited. Many factors can contribute to the stress of raising multiples. Parents may feel in a chronic state of stress and fatigue when caring for multiple infants or toddlers and perhaps another child (or more). The attachment process is more complex. Multiples are more likely to require care for ongoing health issues. Differences in multiples' temperaments may lead to different parental responses to the individual multiples. Although all may contribute to a situation at risk for abuse, none is insurmountable.

The Red Cross and many social service agencies offer parenting classes for first-time parents as well as for those needing help with anger management. Developing a support system also helps. (See the question on page 195 regarding isolation.) There are also crisis hotlines in most cities for parents who feel they are losing control. Individual counseling is helpful for parents who feel as if they could hurt a baby or child, and insurance often covers this expense.

I've just been put on bed rest, but I'm not sure what that really means.

Bed rest can have different meanings depending on the situation. Be prepared to ask your obstetric health-care provider a lot of questions. You'll want to learn what the research shows about bed rest in multiple pregnancies such as yours. Also find out how strict bed rest is to be. What specific living, household, or job-related activities are allowed and which ones definitely are not allowed? How long will bed rest last? How will this affect caring for any other child(ren) or your spouse? Are there some types of exercises you can do to maintain muscle strength and cardiovascular conditioning? Will other treatment, such as tocolytic medication to stop contractions, or monitoring be necessary or will it be affected by bed rest? The provider's answers will vary based on your condition and the degree of caution believed necessary. You probably will think of new questions as you continue on bed rest, and be sure to contact your provider for answers as you think of them.

GLOSSARY

Activity level one trait of temperament. See *behavioral style* and *temperament*.

Alpha-fetoprotein (AFP) a fetal protein that crosses the placenta and into the maternal blood (serum). A blood test drawn during the second trimester in pregnancy, it may be written as MSAFP for *maternal serum alpha-fetoprotein* and is found at higher levels with multiple pregnancies.

Amniotic fluid index (AFI) ultrasound test that helps providers measure and compare the amount of amniotic fluid in each baby's amniotic sac over time, which is of value in certain suspected or diagnosed prenatal conditions.

Amniotic sac the sac surrounding an unborn fetus, composed of two membranes—an inner amnion and outer chorion—lying one on top of another and filled with amniotic fluid. Also referred to as the *bag of waters* or *membranes*.

Assisted reproductive technology (ART) the use of ovarian stimulation and/or medical procedures to increase the likelihood of conception for couples diagnosed with a fertility-related problem.

Attachment the process of forming an enduring relationship. See *bonding*.

Behavioral style the combination of inherited temperament traits resulting in each person's unique behavior pattern.

Biophysical profile (BPP) the use of ultrasound, nonstress testing, placental grading, and amniotic fluid index to examine fetal well-being.

Bonding the process of forming an enduring attachment with each infant twin.

Celebrity syndrome stressing of children's multiple status at the expense of each child's individuality to increase parental celebrity status. Often associated with *unit thinking*.

Cerclage (cervical) a surgical procedure to insert sutures or a band in the cervix that prevents or limits cervical dilation in women who have had recurrent pregnancy loss or preterm delivery due to a condition called incompetent cervix.

Cesarean birth a surgical procedure for delivering an infant through abdominal and uterine incisions. Also called cesarean delivery or cesarean section.

Cobedding the placing of two or more multiples in the same crib, usually in the NICU.

Corticosteroids a medication that is given during an episode of preterm labor to help "speed" fetal lung development.

Differentiation the process of determining differences and similarities between twins. One aspect of the parent-twin(s) attachment process.

Dizygotic twins twins derived from the separate fertilization of two different ova and two different sperm, resulting in two genetically distinct zygotes. Also called *fraternal twins* or *heterozygotic twins*.

Doppler flow study an ultrasound test, also called umbilical cord velocimetry, that allows obstetric care providers to observe blood flow in the babies' umbilical cords.

Embryo transfer placement of an IVF zygote in the uterus. See *in vitro fertilization.*

Estriol (salivary or urine) a test for estrogen (hormone) produced by the placenta, which is found in maternal blood, saliva, and urine, and may provide clues about placenta and fetal well-being.

Family bed the meeting of infants' or young children's nighttime needs for feeding and/or cuddling by allowing them to share their parents' bed for all or part of the night.

Fertility drugs see *ovulatory induction agents.*

Fertilization the union of a sperm and ovum in which their combined genetic material results in a new single cell called a zygote.

Fetal fibronectin (fFn) a test for protein normally present in vaginal secretions before the 22nd week of pregnancy but absent in secretions from the 22nd to 36th week and used to help predict both the likelihood or unlikelihood of preterm labor.

Fetal Growth Restriction (FGR) a weight in an unborn fetus below the tenth percentile for within normal range of normal weight for gestational age, also referred to as *Intrauterine Growth Restriction* (IUGR).

Fetal monitor a method for monitoring fetal heart rate (FHR).

Fetal surveillance the use of screening or testing methods to monitor the fetus's well-being.

Flip-flopping the alternating, or taking turns, of a particular behavior(s) by twins.

Gamete intrafallopian transfer (GIFT) surgical placement of ovum (or ova) and sperm in a fallopian tube for fertilization.

Gestation a term for the duration of pregnancy, which in humans normally lasts 38 to 42 weeks.

Gonadotropins hormonal agents used to stimulate follicle (egg/ovum) development in the ovaries.

Heterozygotic twins see *dizygotic twins.*

Higher-order multiples three or more individuals conceived or born as part of a set of multiples, also referred to as supertwins.

High risk a pregnancy with the potential for developing one or more complications.

Homozygotic twins see *monozygotic twins.*

Human chorionic gonadotropin (hCG) a hormone secreted by the embryo from early pregnancy, which rises as pregnancy progresses and is found at higher levels for weeks of pregnancy with multiple pregnancies, and may be referred to as MShCG for *maternal serum human chorionic gonadotropin.*

Human placental lactogen (HPL) a hormone produced by the placenta that crosses into the mother's blood (serum), providing clues about placental function, and may be referred to as MSHPL for *maternal serum human placental lactogen.*

Hyperemesis gravidarum a severe or prolonged vomiting during pregnancy that can interfere with adequate hydration and weight gain.

Idioglossia the rare development of a unique, private language understood only by the children involved.

Incompetent cervix a painless dilation of the cervix, usually during the second trimester of pregnancy, resulting in pregnancy loss.

201

Intrauterine growth restriction (IUGR) see *fetal growth restriction.*

Intrauterine insemination (IUI) the direct placement of sperm in the uterus via a catheter, often used in addition to ovarian stimulation, to increase the likelihood of conception for specific fertility-related problems.

In vitro fertilization (IVF) fertilization of an ovum in a laboratory rather than within a woman's fallopian tube.

Kangaroo care skin-to-skin care in which one or two preterm babies are placed in direct skin contact on a parent's chest, with the baby (babies) usually dressed in only a diaper and cap.

Kick count sometimes called *fetal activity count,* a recording of the number of movements the babies make for a specific hour each day during the last 12 (twins) or 15 (higher-order multiples) weeks of pregnancy, providing a clue to fetal well-being.

Low birth weight (LBW) a birth weight of less than 5 pounds, 8 ounces.

Monozygotic twins twins derived from the fertilization of a single ovum and sperm, resulting in one zygote that subsequently divides into two zygotes sharing the same genetic material. See also *identical homozygotic twins.*

Multifetal reduction a procedure that decreases the number of fetuses in a higher-order multiple pregnancy.

Newborn intensive care unit (NICU) a nursery that has special equipment and trained staff members to closely monitor premature or sick newborns. Also called a neonatal intensive care nursery or a special care nursery (SCN).

Nonstress test (NST) measures the response of each fetus's heart rate to fetal movement through the use of an external electronic fetal monitor (EFM), providing clues about the fetuses' well-being.

Ovarian stimulation the promotion of the maturation of more than one egg (follicle/ovum) per menstrual cycle by ovulatory induction agent medication or gonadotropins.

Ovulatory induction agents hormonal treatment facilitating the maturation and ovulation, or release, of ova. Also referred to as *fertility drugs.*

Placenta the organ in contact with the mother's uterine wall through which oxygen and nutrients for the fetus are exchanged for fetal waste products to be eliminated through the maternal physical systems. Also called the *afterbirth*.

Placental grading a test that checks for calcifications associated with placenta "aging."

Preeclampsia see *pregnancy-induced hypertension*.

Pregnancy-induced hypertension (PIH) a condition typified by the sudden appearance of high blood pressure, protein in the urine, and fluid retention causing body swelling, which can result in headaches and/or seeing spots, pain above the stomach area, and/or convulsions. Also referred to as *preeclampsia* or *toxemia* of pregnancy.

Prematurity the birth of an infant before 37 weeks of gestation, which is associated with immaturity of the infant's physical systems and low birth weight.

Preterm delivery the birth of an infant before 37 weeks of gestation. Also called *premature delivery*.

Preterm labor the onset of labor before 37 weeks of gestation. Also called *premature labor*.

Respiratory Syncytial Virus (RSV) a leading cause of lower respiratory tract infections in infants and young children. Usually a minor illness, it may cause very serious symptoms in any infant that was preterm or high-risk at birth.

Small for gestational age (SGA) a decrease in the weight/length ratio of a fetus compared with normal parameters for gestational age. Can be related to *intrauterine growth retardation*.

Sonogram see *ultrasound scan*.

Supertwins see *higher-order multiples*.

Tocolytics medications used to suppress, slow, or halt preterm labor to delay or postpone delivery.

Toxemia see *pregnancy-induced hypertension*.

Transfusion syndrome a condition that can occur only when monozygotic twins share a placenta. The result of blood vessel-to-vessel connections within their placenta leading to a disproportionate amount of oxygen and nutrients reaching one twin.

Twin personality a third distinct personality, different from either twin, but resulting from their combined energies.

Twinskin the looseness and puckered appearance of the abdominal skin after some twin pregnancies. Improves to varying degrees with time and exercise.

Ultrasound scan an instrument using sound waves to "see" the fetus within the uterus. Also referred to as a *sonogram*.

Unit bonding the formation of an attachment to twins as a single unit rather than to the individuals within a twin set.

Unit thinking the consideration of twins as a single entity.

Zygosity refers to twin set's origin as two separate zygotes or one zygote that completely splits during cell division. See *dizygotic twins* and *monozygotic twins*.

Appendix A

SUGGESTED READING

Books

Parenting Multiple-Birth Children

Agnew, C.L., Klein, A.H., Ganon, J.A., & Robert, V. *Twins!: Expert Advice from Two Practicing Physicians on Pregnancy, Birth, and the First Year.* New York: HarperCollins, 1997.

Albi, L., Johnson, D., Catlin, D., Deurloo, D.F., & Greatwood, S. *Mothering Twins: From Hearing the News to Beyond the Terrible Twos.* New York: Fireside (Simon & Schuster), 1993.

Bowers, N. *The Multiple Pregnancy Sourcebook.* Los Angeles, CA: Lowell House, 2001, in press.

Bryan, E.M. *Twins and Higher Multiple Births: A Guide to Their Nature and Nurture.* London, England: Edward Arnold, 1992.

Clegg, A. & Woolett, A. *Twins: From Conception to Five Years.* New York: Ballantine Books, 1983.

Collier, H.L. *The Psychology of Twins: A Practical Handbook for Parents of Multiples* (rev. ed.) Englewood, CO: Twins Magazine, 1996.

Friedrich, E. & Rowland, C. *The Parents' Guide to Raising Twins.* St. Martin's Press, 1990.

Gromada, K.K. *Mothering Multiples: Breastfeeding and Caring for Twins or More!* (rev. ed.). Schaumburg, IL: La Leche League International, 1999.

Luke, B. & Eberlein, T. *When You're Expecting Twins, Triplets, or Quads: A Complete Resource.* New York: HarperPerennial Library, 1999.

Malmstrom, P.M. & Poland, J. *The Art of Parenting Multiples: The Unique Joys and Challenges of Raising Twins and Other Multiples.* New York: Ballantine Books, 1999.

Noble, E. *Having Twins*, 2nd ed. Boston: Houghton-Mifflin, 1992.

Novotny, P.P. *The Joy of Twins and Other Multiple Births: Having, Raising, and Loving Babies Who Arrive in Groups* (rev. ed.). New York: Crown Publishers, 1994.

Pearlman, E.M. & Ganon, J.A. *Raising Twins: What Parents Want to Know (and What Twins Want to Tell Them)*. New York: HarperCollins, 2000.

Rothbart, B. *Multiple Blessings: From Pregnancy Through Childhood, a Guide for Parents of Twins, Triplets, or More*. New York: Hearst, 1994.

Tinglof, C.B. *Double Duty: The Parents' Guide to Raising Twins, from Pregnancy Through the School Years*. Chicago, IL: Contemporary Books, 1998.

By or Especially for Parents of Higher-Order Multiples

Brevington, F. *Make Way for Triplets*. Mesa, AZ: Triple Treat Publications, 1992.

Dilley, B., Dilley, K., & Stall, S. *Special Delivery: How We Are Raising America's Only Sextuplets ... and Loving It*. Thorpe, F.A. Ltd., 1996.

Hall, J.P. & Hall, D. *The Stork Brought Three: Our Epic Journey as Parents of Triplets*. Englewood, CO: Twins Magazine, 1997.

Laut, W., Laut, S., & Benit, K. *Raising Multiple Birth Children: A Parents' Survival Guide*. Worcester, MA: Chandler House Press, 1999.

McCaughey, K., McCaughey, B., Lewis, D., & Lewis, G. *Seven from Heaven*. Nashville, TN: Thomas Nelson, 1998.

Psychology

Ainslie, R.C. *The Psychology of Twinship*. Northvale, NJ: Jason Aronson, 1997.

Segal, N.L. *Entwined Lives: Twins and What They Teach Us About Human Behavior*. New York: E.P. Dutton, 1999.

Stewart, E.A. *Exploring Twins: Towards a Social Analysis of Twinship*. New York: St. Martin's Press, 2000.

Wright, L. *Twins: And What They Tell Us About Who We Are.* New York: John Wiley, 1997.

Twins on Twins

Ganz, D., Ganz, L., Tresmowski, A., & Balkenberg, B. *The Book of Twins: A Celebration in Words and Pictures.* New York: Delacorte Press, 1998.

Sandweiss, R., Sandweiss, R., & Fields, D. *Twins.* Philadelphia: Running Press, 1998.

Sipes, J.S. & Sipes, N.J. *Dancing Naked in Front of the Fridge.* Lions Bay, British Columbia: FairWinds Press, 1999.

Periodicals

International Society for Twin Studies (ISTS): Council of Multiple Birth Organizations (COMBO) (1998). *Declaration of Rights and Statement of Needs of Twins and Higher-Order Multiples. Twin Research, 1*(1), 52–56; Available online: *www.ists.qimr. edu.au/Rights.html*

Twins Magazine, 5350 S. Roslyn, Suite 400, Englewood, CO 80111-2125; phone: 888/55-TWINS (89467) or 800/328-3211 or 303/729-1000; fax: 303/290–9025; e-mail: *twins.editor@businessword.com*; web site: *www.twinsmagazine.com*

(Membership in many associations for parents of multiples includes a subscription to an informational newsletter. See Appendix B.)

Videotapes

Double Duty: The Joys and Challenges of Caring for Newborn Twins (1998) (30 minutes) (15-minute edited version available). Two by Two, 6014 Lattimer, Houston, TX 77035; phone: 713/721-9026; fax: 713/721-0951 (personal or health-care agency licensed copy) or InJoy Productions, Inc., 3970 Broadway, Suite B-4, Boulder, CO 80301; phone: 800-326-2082 or 303/447-2082; fax: 303-449-8788 (licensed copy).

Your Multiples and You, Conception to Six Months (27 minutes) and *Your Multiples and You—Toddlers and Preschoolers* (45 minutes). NOMOTC, P.O. Box 23188, Albuquerque, NM 87192-1188; e-mail: *NOMOTC@aol.com*; web site: *www.nomotc.org*

General Books

Growth and Development

Brazelton, T.B. *Infants and Mothers: Differences in Development* (rev. ed.). New York: Delacorte Press, 1994.

Faber, A. & Maslish, E. *Siblings Without Rivalry: How to Help Your Children Live Together So You Can Live Too* (rev. ed.). New York: Avon, 1998.

Leach, P. *Your Baby and Child: From Birth to Age Five* (rev. ed.). New York: Knopf, 1997.

Sears, W. & Sears, M. *The Baby Book: Everything You Need to Know About Your Baby from Birth to Age Two.* New York: Little Brown & Co, 1993.

White, B. *The New First Three Years of Life* (20th rev. ed.). New York: Fireside (Simon & Schuster), 1995.

General Breastfeeding

Huggins, K. *The Nursing Mother's Companion*, 4th ed. Boston, MA: Harvard Common Press, 1999.

La Leche League International (LLLI). *The Womanly Art of Breastfeeding*, 7th ed. Schaumburg, IL: LLLI, 1997.

Sears, W. & Sears, M. *The Breastfeeding Book: Everything You Need to Know About Nursing Your Child from Birth Through Weaning.* New York: Little Brown & Co, 2000.

Spangler, A.K. *Breastfeeding: A Parent's Guide* (rev. ed.). P.O. Box 501046, Atlanta: GA 31150-1046: Author, 1999.

Premature Babies

Linden, D.W., Paroli, E.T., & Doron, M.W. *Preemies: The Essential Guide for Parents of Premature Babies.* New York: Pocket Books, 2000.

SUGGESTED READING
Tracy, A.E. & Bernbaum, J.C. (Eds.) with Maroney, D.I. & Groothuis, J.R. *Your Premature Baby and Child: Helpful Answers and Advice for Parents*. New York: Berkley Publishing Group, 1999.

Sleep

Eberlein, T. *Sleep: How to Teach Your Child to Sleep Like a Baby*. New York: Pocket Books, 1996.

Ferber, R. *Solving Your Child's Sleep Problems*. New York: Simon & Schuster, 1986.

Gottlieb, S. *Keys to Children's Sleep Problems*. Hauppauge, NY: Barron's, 1993.

Sears, W. *Nighttime Parenting* (rev. ed.). Schaumburg, IL: LLLI, 1999.

Thevenin, T. *The Family Bed: An Age-Old Concept in Childrearing* (rev.). Wayne, NJ: Avery, 1987.

Appendix B

~~~~~~

RESOURCES

North American Associations for Parents of Multiples

Asociación de Nacimientos Multiples, A.C. (Mexico);
phone: +52 (4) 212.60.50 & 212.60.44;
e-mail: agemelos@mail.intermex.com.mx;
web site: www.gemelos.org.mx:

National Online Fathers of Twins Club, www.nofotc.org

National Organization of Mothers of Twins Clubs, Inc.
(NOMOTC); e-mail: NOMOTC@aol.com;
web site: www.nomotc.org/

Parents of Multiple Births Association of Canada
(POMBA/Association des Parents de Naissances Multiples du
Canada); phone: 905/888-0725, e-mail: office@pomba.org;
web site: www.pomba.org/

North American Associations for Parents of Higher-Order Multiples

Mothers of Super Twins (MOST); phone: 631/859-1110;
e-mail: Maureen@MOSTonline.org; web site: www.MOSTonline.org/

Single Triplet Moms Network; phone: 318/235-7697

The Triplet Connection; phone: 209/474-0885;
e-mail: tc@tripletconnection.org;
web site: www.tripletconnection.org/

Triplets, Quads, & Quints Association (Canada);
e-mail: diane@tqq.com; web site: www.tqq.com/

Childbirth Preparation Classes for Multiple Birth

Marvelous Multiples, Inc.; phone: 770/242-2750;
e-mail: marvmult@aol.com;
web page: www.marvelousmultiples.com/

Grief Support: Miscarriage or Death of a Multiple(s)

Center for Loss in Multiple Birth, Inc. (CLIMB);
phone: 907/222-5321; e-mail: climb@pobox.alaska.net;
web site: www.climb-support.org/

Twinless Twins International Support Group (for multiples who
have experienced the death of a comultiple); phone: 219/627-5414;
e-mail: twinless@iserv.net; web site: www.fwi.com/twinless/

Home Schooling Multiples

Home School Families of Twins (information, support,
newsletter); phone: 972/234-6818; e-mail: margie.hsft@juno.com;
web site: home.flash.net/~hsft/

Twin-to-Twin Transfusion Syndrome (and Other Twin-related Health Issues)

Twin Hope, Inc.; phone: 216/228-TTTS (8887);
e-mail: twinhope@twinhope.com;
web site: www.twinhope.com/twinhope.html

Twin-to-Twin Transfusion Syndrome Foundation, Inc.;
voice mail: 440/899-TTTS (8887); e-mail: info@tttsfoundation.org;
web site: www.tttsfoundation.org/

Other Multiples-related Organizations: Information, Research, Festivals

Center for the Study of Multiple Birth, 333 E. Superior St., Suite
464, Chicago, IL 60611; phone: 312/266-9093;
e-mail: lgk395@nwu.edu; web site: www.multiplebirth.com/

The Twins Foundation (twin registry); phone: 401/729-1000;
e-mail: twins@twinsfoundation.com;
web site: www.twinsfoundation.com/

Twins Days Festival (world's largest annual gathering of multiples); phone: 330/425-3652; e-mail: info@twinsdays.org; web site: www.twinsworld.com/

Twin Services (parent support; Spanish information also); phone: 510/524-0863; e-mail: twinservices@juno.com; web site: www.twinservices.org/

Helpful Organizations

(Many USA organizations provide referral/links to international organizations.)

Bed Rest/High-risk Pregnancy

Sidelines National Support Network; phone: 949/497-2265; e-mail: sidelines@sidelines.org; web site: www.sidelines.org/

Birth and Postpartum Support: Doulas

DONA (Doulas of North America); phone: 801/756-7331; e-mail: askDONA@aol.com; web site: www.dona.com/

Breastfeeding/Lactation

La Leche League International; phone: 847/519-7730 or 800-LALECHE; e-mail: lllhq@llli.org; web site: http://www.lalecheleague.org/

International Lactation Consultant Association (IBCLC referral); phone: 919/787-5181; e-mail: ilca@erols.com; web site: www.ilca.org/

Breastfeeding.com (illustrations/photographs of simultaneous breastfeeding positions); web site: www.breastfeeding.com/helpme/helpme_images_twins.html

Child Safety and Poison Control—USA

American Association of Poison Control Centers; phone 202/362-7217; e-mail: aapcc@poison.org; web site: www.aapcc.org/

U.S. Consumer Product Safety Commission (CPSC);
phone: 800/638-2772; e-mail: info@cpsc.gov;
web site: www.cpsc.gov/

Children/Multiples with Special Needs—USA

March of Dimes Birth Defects Foundation; phone: 888-MODIMES
(663-4637; USA toll-free) or 001-914-997-4765 (from outside USA);
e-mail: educationservices@modimes.org;
web site: www.modimes.org/

Infant Care Classes—USA

American Red Cross (local referral); phone: 703/248-4222;
e-mail: info@usa.redcross.org;
web site: www.redcross.org/index.shtml

Infertility Support and Information—USA

Resolve, Inc. (local chapter referral); phone: 617/623-0744
(HelpLine), 617/623-1156; e-mail: resolveinc@aol.com;
web site: www.resolve.org/

Postpartum Depression or Anxiety Disorders—USA

Depression After Delivery, Inc.; phone: 800/944-4PPD (773)
(information request line) or 215/295-3994 (professional inquiries);
web site: www.behavenet.com/dadinc/

Postpartum Support International (postpartum depression or
anxiety disorder information); phone: 805/967-7636;
e-mail: thonikman@compuserv.com;
web site: www.chss.iup.edu/postpartum/

Perinatal Dietitians—USA

American Dietetic Association (local referral);
phone: 800/877-1600 or 312/899-0040 (Chicago) or
202/371-0500 (Washington, DC); e-mail: hotline@eatright.org;
web site: www.eatright.org/

Preterm Birth Support—USA

American Association for Premature Infants (AAPI);
e-mail: feedback@aapi-online.org; web site: www.aapi-online.org

Helpful Products

Breastfeeding Aids

Double Blessings (EZ-2-Nurse twins breastfeeding pillow); phone:
800/584-TWIN (8946); e-mail: info@doubleblessings.com;
web site: www.doubleblessings.com/index.html

Hollister Ameda-Egnell (hospital-grade, self-cycling breast pump
purchase or rental, double collection kit, etc.), Hollister,
Incorporated; phone: 800/323-4060 (USA) or
800/263-7400 (Canada); web site: www.hollister.com/

INFACT Canada ("Table for Two" poster, twins breastfeeding
simultaneously); phone: 416/595-9819; e-mail: infact@ftn.net;
web site: www.infactcanada.ca/resources/2nd_poster2.htm

Medela, Inc. (hospital-grade, self-cycling breast pump purchase or
rental, double collection kit, electronic scale rental, alternative
feeding devices, etc.); phone: 800/435-8316;
web site: www.medela.com/

Motherwear (fashions for discreet breastfeeding);
phone: 800/950-2500 (USA or Canada) or
413/586-3488 (other countries); e-mail: info@motherwear.com;
web site: www.motherwear.com/

The Nurturing Mother's Boutique (twin nursing pillow, POM
books/video); phone: 920/231-1611 or 888/666-7224;
e-mail: toman@momsbags.com; web site: www.momsbags.com/

DNA-Zygosity Testing

Affiliated Genetics, Inc. (cheek swab kit and DNA analysis;
worldwide mailing); phone: 801/298-3366;
e-mail: btanner@burgoyne.com;
web site: www.affiliatedgenetics.com/

Proactive Genetics, Inc. (cheek swab kit and DNA analysis);
phone: 781/639-5126; e-mail: info@proactivegenetics.com;
web site: www.proactivegenetics.com/

Prenatal/Postpartum Pelvic Support

Loving Comfort Maternity Support, c/o CMO, Incorporated;
phone: 800/344-0011 or 330/745-9679;
e-mail: support@cmo-inc.com;
web site: www.maternitysupport.com/

Mom-Ez Maternity Support, c/o Smith Orthopedics;
phone: 800/279-7711; e-mail: office@smithorthopedics.com;
web site: www.smithorthopedics.com/

Prenatal Cradle, Inc.; phone: 800/607-3572;
e-mail: prenatal@htonline.com;
web site: www.l-n.com/prenatalcradle/index.html

Slings/Carriers

Gemini Carrier (twins) and *MaxiMom* carrier (twins or triplets),
Tot Tenders, Inc.; phone: 800/634-6870;
e-mail: tottenders@proaxis.com; web site: www.babycarriers.com

Over the Shoulder Baby Holder (OTSBH) (multiples discount), c/o
Parent's Pal; phone: 770/396-4747;
e-mail: parentspal@mindspring.com; web site:
www.parentspal.com/ and *Breastfeeding.com*
(photographs of OTSBH use with twins):
www.breastfeeding.com/shopping/otsbh/otsbh_how_to_twins.html

Strollers and Prams: Double to Quadruple

Baby Jogger; phone: 800/241-1848 or 509/457-0925;
e-mail: support@babyjogger.com;
web sites: www.babyjogger.com or
www.babyjogger.com/international.htm (international distributors)

Inglesina USA, Inc.; phone: 877/486-5112 (toll-free);
e-mail: inglesina@comcastwork.net;
web site (products & distributors by country): www.inglesina.com/

Maclaren USA, Inc.; phone: 877/442-4622 or 203/354-4400;
e-mail: info@maclarenbaby.com;
web site (products & distributors by country):
www.maclarenstrollers.com/

Peg-Perego, USA; phone: 800/671-1701 or 219/482-8191 or 800/225-1558 (Spanish-speaking); e-mail: peregoservice@perego.com;
web site: www.perego.com/ (contacts for Canada and International)

Runabout Minivan (double, triple, and quadruple models), see
MOST General Store or Triplet Products Mall below.

Web Sites: General Shopping for Multiples-Related Products

Multiples Mall (links to sites with products or resources);
e-mail: mary.shepherd@home.com;
web site: www.multiplesmall.com/

More Than One, Inc. or *Mainly Multiples* (subsidiary);
phone: 800/388-TWIN (8946); web site: www.morethan1.com/ or
www-morethan1-com/mmcover.htm/

Multiple Trends; phone: 800/567-9559;
e-mail: info@multipletrends.com;
web site: www.multipletrends.com/

MOST General Store (Mothers of Supertwins):
www.mostonline.org/store/index.htm/

Triplet Products Mall (Triplet Connection):
www.tripletconnection.org/tripmall.html

TwinsMall (Twins Magazine):
www.twinsmagazine.com/ twinsmall.shtml

Twinshopping.com (new/pre-owned), P.O. Box 6056 New York, NY
10128; phone: 800/RU TWINS (78 89467) or 212/289-1777;
web site: www.twinshopping.com/

INDEX

217